THE LIFE OF
CHARLES THOMSON

SECRETARY OF THE CONTINENTAL CONGRESS
AND TRANSLATOR OF THE BIBLE FROM THE GREEK

2nd Edition

LEWIS R. HARLEY, PH.D.

SUNBURY
PRESS
Mechanicsburg, PA USA

Published by Sunbury Press, Inc.
Mechanicsburg, Pennsylvania

SUNBURY
P R E S S
www.sunburypress.com

For information about special discounts for bulk purchases, please contact Sunbury Press Orders Dept. at (855) 338-8359 or orders@sunburypress.com.

To request one of our authors for speaking engagements or book signings, please contact Sunbury Press Publicity Dept. at publicity@sunburypress.com.

SECOND SUNBURY PRESS EDITION: December 2020

Set in Adobe Garamond | Interior design by Crystal Devine | Cover by Lawrence Knorr | Edited by Lawrence Knorr.

Publisher's Cataloging-in-Publication Data
Names: Harley, Lewis R., author.
Title: The life of Charles Thomson / Lewis R. Harley, Ph.D.
Description: Second trade paperback edition. | Mechanicsburg, PA : Sunbury Press, 2020.
Summary: Biography of Charles Thomson, the secretary of the Continental Congress from its founding until the elections following the passage of the US Constituion. Thomson was the second person to sign the Declaration of Independence, attesting to John Hancock's signature.
Identifiers: ISBN 978-1-620064-65-8 (softcover).
Subjects: BIOGRAPHY & AUTOBIOGRAPHY / Political | HISTORY / United States / Revolutionary Period (1775-1800) | HISTORY / US History / Mid-Atlantic.

Product of the United States of America
0 1 1 2 3 5 8 13 21 34 55

Continue the Enlightenment!

To
My Father and Mother
I Dedicate This Book

Contents

Foreword

The name Charles Thomson is not widely known among the Founding Fathers of the United States of America. This is despite his role as the Secretary of the Continental Congress for its entire duration. Before the adoption of the US Constitution, the Congress governed the nation. The President of Congress and the Secretary of Congress were important figures. Fourteen different men served in the role of President of Congress from 1774 to 1788, before the creation of the role of President of the United States. The most famous was probably John Hancock, who penned his name boldly on the Declaration of Independence. Few know that it was Thomson who helped edit the document, was the first to read it aloud, arranged for its distribution and printing, and affixed his name as the only other signer of the original document on July 4, 1776. Of course, the delegates signed the document the following month. Thomson signed as Secretary and not as a delegate. For that reason, he does not appear on many lists of the Signers of the Declaration of Independence.

Perhaps the role of Secretary of the Continental Congress has not been fully appreciated by historians. There may be good reason for this. Thomson, who kept copious records and was seen by many as the official word of the government, also destroyed his personal journals rather than write what would have been the most comprehensive, objective, and honest portrayal of the proceedings of the government during the Revolution. In many ways, Thomson was "the man who knew too much." He did not want to dishonor any of the other patriots or their families. Ultimately, he thought it best to cast his books into the fire.

As you will see in Harley's biography from 1900, Thomson was also involved in intellectual pursuits. He was a member of the American Philosophical Society and close friends with both Benjamin Franklin and Thomas Jefferson. Thomson was always curious about science and the natural world.

Thomson was also a religious man and had many conversations with Jefferson on the subject. Thomson was an expert in early languages and translated the New Testament from Greek. It was this deep religious belief that guided his conversation with Jefferson about slavery. In his letter to Jefferson on November 2, 1785, Thomson wrote:

Dear Sir   New York, Novr. 2, 1785[1]

I have received your several favours of Feby 8 June 21 and July 14 and also a copy of your Notes by Mr. Houdon, for which I am much obliged. It grieves me to the soul that there should be such just grounds for your apprehensions respecting the irritation that will be produced in the southern states by what you have said of slavery. However I would not have you discouraged. This is a cancer that we must get rid of. It is a blot in our character that must be wiped out. If it cannot be done by religion, reason, and philosophy, confident I am that it will one day be by blood. I confess I am more afraid of this than of the Algerine piracies or the jealousy entertained of us by European powers of which we hear so much of late. However I have the satisfaction to find that philosophy is gaining ground of selfishness in this respect. If this can be rooted out, and our land filled with freemen, union preserved and the spirit of liberty maintained and cherished I think in 25 or 30 years we shall have nothing to fear from the rest of the world.

---

1. "To Thomas Jefferson from Charles Thomson, 2 November 1785," *The Papers of Thomas Jefferson*, vol. 9, 1 November 1785–22 June 1786, ed. Julian P. Boyd. Princeton: Princeton University Press, 1954, pp. 9–10.

Mr. Houdon has been to Mount Vernon and taken the Bust of our Amiable General. He exhibited it to the view of Congress. It appears to me to [be] executed in a masterly manner. I acknowledge my want of skill to judge of performances of this nature. But there is in the air and attitude of this something that pleases me. Most other pictures seem to have their attention turned on the objects around them; but in this the Artist by elevating the chin and countenance has given it the air of one looking forward into futurity. But I will not venture any criticisms for fear of betraying my ignorance. Our good old friend Dr. F. is arrived safe and well and honoured with the chair of President of Pensylvania. All parties concurred in the choice. I hope it will be comfortable as it is honorable. As to matters within my circle they jog on as usual. Though many occurrences have happened which would be subject of conversation, there are few worth troubling you with in a letter. As to public matters I take it for granted you are well informed through the proper channel. You see by the journal that the duties of my office are much enlarged.

I am with great esteem & regard Dear Sir Your affectionate friend & Servt.,

Chas. Thomson

Despite Mrs. Thomson's Harrison ancestors owning considerable slaves, he was not himself a slaveowner. Based on his discourse with Jefferson, Thomson was against the institution. He also accurately predicted a Civil War would be necessary to end it.

Charles Thomson may very well have been the smartest and most congenial of all the Founding Fathers. It was he who was sent to General George Washington at Mount Vernon to inform him of his election to the presidency. At that point, Thomson's public career was over. As you will see, a full life followed.

—Lawrence Knorr (2020)

Preface

This book was a monograph of forty-two pages in its original form, which I prepared for the Historical Society of Montgomery County, Pennsylvania. After its publication in the Society's Collections two years ago, I decided to write a more comprehensive biography of Charles Thomson. His distinguished public services in the Revolutionary period, and his devotion to Biblical literature after he had retired to private life, render no apology necessary for the appearance of this work.

As Secretary of the Continental Congress, Thomson had gathered much valuable information to write a history of his times. He destroyed nearly all his papers in his declining years, leaving only those mentioned in this volume's Bibliography. I have thus been compelled to depend chiefly upon these sources for my material. Thomson's correspondence with Franklin and Jefferson, and his papers in the *New York Historical Society collections for the year 1878*, throw considerable light on his relations with the Continental Congress. He was one of the best scholars of his day, and after retiring from public life in 1789, he devoted twenty-five years to the translation of the Bible from the Greek and to *A Synopsis of the Four Evangelists*. John F. Watson was well acquainted with Thomson and frequently visited him at Harriton. His account of the venerable scholar in the Annals of Philadelphia and Pennsylvania has been consulted in preparing the closing part of this biography. Thomson's manuscripts and notes on the study of the Scriptures give evidence of a vigorous, cultivated mind and show how constant was his application to this favorite employment.

I wish to express my thanks to Hon. Samuel W. Pennypacker, of Philadelphia, who first suggested to me the writing of this book. He has long been regarded as the chief authority on Pennsylvania history, and he has done much to direct students to its sources.

I am under obligations to Samuel K. Chambers, Esq., of West Grove, Pa., for his valuable assistance in gathering information concerning the New London Academy and Thomson's school life there.

My thanks are due to Joseph Fornance, Esq., of Norristown, Pa., Mr. Howard Edwards, of Philadelphia, and Mr. Gilbert Cope, of West Chester, Pa., for valuable suggestions. Grateful acknowledgment is made to Miss Caroline G. Thomson, and Mrs. Henry Barnes, of Philadelphia, and Mrs. Clara C. Kerr, of Newark, Delaware, descendants of Charles Thomson's brother, Alexander, for important facts relating to the family.

I have to thank Henry C. Conrad, Esq., Librarian of the Historical Society of Delaware, Dr. I. Minis Hays, Librarian of the American Philosophical Society, and Gregory B. Keen, A. M., Librarian of the Historical Society of Pennsylvania, for the many courtesies extended to me during the preparation of this book.

—Lewis R. Harley (1900)
The Central High School, Philadelphia

chapter one

Early Life

While the historian has done ample justice to the memory of the Fathers of the Republic, the patriotic services of Charles Thomson have been but slightly treated by even the most impartial writers. In every critical epoch of history, there are two forces at work—the one attracting the country's admiration by superior statesmanship or thrilling deeds of valor on the battlefield; the other a steady influence guiding the destinies of the state in the hour of peril. Charles Thomson is a representative of this latter force. To the hero worshipper, the Secretary of the Continental Congress might not prove a very inspiring subject. At the first casual glance, the clerk at his desk noting down the transactions of the Congress of the Colonies is too ordinary a personage to crowd himself upon the attention of the historian; but this was only a small portion of Thomson's services in our early political history. A finished scholar, he brought good judgment into public life; an ardent patriot, he labored incessantly to strengthen the sentiment for independence in Pennsylvania, a skillful organizer, he aided powerfully to hold together the discordant factions of the Continental Congress; in the retirement of private life, he made a valuable contribution to Biblical literature; of a vigorous constitution, he lived to see the struggling Colonies become a powerful Republic, and he died at a good old age at the very time when Lafayette was making his tour throughout the United States.

Charles Thomson was born in the town of Gortede, parish Maharan, County Derry, Ireland, the first week in November 1729. He was the son of John Thomson, one of the most respectable men of Ulster. Our subject's birth occurred when Protestant emigration was robbing Ireland of thousands of her best people. More than twenty thousand left Ulster and settled along the Atlantic seaboard on the destruction of the woolen trade and the Test Act's enforcement. Froude says:

> And so, the emigration continued. The young, the courageous, the energetic, the earnest, those alone among her colonists who, if ever Ireland was to be a Protestant country, could be effective missionaries, were torn up by the roots, flung out, and bid find a home elsewhere; and they found a home to which England fifty years later had to regret that she allowed them to be driven.[1]

Most of these immigrants sought a home in Pennsylvania, attracted by the reports of its great natural wealth, and by the fact that under the charter of Penn and the laws of the Province, they could enjoy civil and religious liberty. Before 1726, six thousand had arrived, while the failure of Ulster's crops increased the volume of immigration to twelve thousand a year until 1750.[2] They were nearly all Presbyterians in their church relations, and "they sought an asylum from Church and State intolerance and oppression, if it were to be had only in the wilderness of another continent."[3]

This great body of immigrants aroused the fears of the colonial authorities, and in 1729, James Logan wrote:

> "It looks as if Ireland is to send all her inhabitants hither; for last week not less than six ships arrived, and every day two or three

1. *The English in Ireland in the Eighteenth Century* by James Anthony Froude, Vol. I., p. 394.
2. *A History of the Presbyterian Churches in the United States,* by Robert Ellis Thompson, S. T. D., p. 23.
3. *A Tribute to the Principles, Virtues, Habits and Public Usefulness of the Irish and Scotch Early Settlers in Pennsylvania* by a Descendant, p. 7.

arrive also. The common fear is, that if they continue to come, they will make themselves proprietors of the province."[4]

John Thomson, having been left a widower with six small children, William, Matthew, Alexander, Charles, John, and Mary, determined to make a home for them in America. They set sail from Ireland in 1739, expecting to locate in Pennsylvania. The father was attacked with a violent sickness on the voyage, and dying within sight of the shore, was cast into the ocean near the capes of the Delaware. His expiring prayer was: "God take them up." The death scene was always very affecting to Charles, and referring to the occasion, he once said: "I stood by the bedside of my expiring and much-loved father, closed his eyes and performed the last filial duties to him." The children were now left to the mercy of the sea captain, who embezzled the money the father had brought with him, while they were turned on shore at New Castle. Their fate was a common one to thousands of immigrants at that time. The ordinary vessel of the eighteenth century was a pest-house of disease and misery. Mittelberger, in his *Journey to Pennsylvania in 1750*, describes the sufferings that the Germans endured in crossing the Atlantic as follows:

> It is not, however, till the ship has raised its anchor for the last
> time and started on its eight, nine, ten, eleven, or twelve weeks'
> sail for Philadelphia that the greatest misery is experienced. Then
> there are heartrending scenes! The filth and stench of the vessels
> no pen could describe, while the diverse diseases, sea-sickness in
> every form, headache, biliousness, constipation, dysentery, scarlet
> fever, scrofula, cancers, etc., caused by the miserable salt food and
> the vile drinking water are truly deplorable, not to speak of the
> deaths which occur on every side.
>
> It is little wonder that so many of the passengers are seized
> with sickness and disease, for, in addition to all their other
> hardships and miseries, they have cooked food only three times

---

4. In 1729, the year of Thomson's birth, 4500 passengers and servants from Ireland, arrived at New Castle. See Holmes' *American Annals*, Vol. 2, p. 123.

a week, and this (it is always of a decidedly inferior quality, and served in very small quantities) is so filthy that the very sight of it is loathsome. Moreover, the drinking water is so black, thick, and full of worms that it makes one shudder to look at it, and even those suffering the tortures of thirst frequently find it almost impossible to swallow it.

This account is also true regarding the sufferings and privations of the Irish immigrants. They were plundered and ill-treated, while the infamous redemption system reduced thousands to a miserable condition.

On landing at New Castle, the Thomson children were separated, and it is quite possible that they were bound to serve as redemptioners.[5] According to some authorities, William drifted to South Carolina, and in the Revolutionary War, distinguished himself by his great bravery. Alexander became a prosperous farmer near New Castle, and many descendants of his son John, are still living in Newark, Delaware, and Philadelphia. Charles resided for a time with a blacksmith's family at New Castle, who thought of having him indented as an apprentice. John F. Watson relates:

He chanced to overhear them speaking on this design one night, and determining from the vigor of his mind, that he should devote himself to better business, he arose in the night and made his escape with his little all packed upon his back. As he trudged the road, not knowing whither he went, it was his chance or providence in the case, to be overtaken by a traveling lady of the neighborhood, who, entering into conversation with him, asked him 'what he would like to be in future life.' He promptly answered that he should like to be a scholar or gain his support by his mind and pen. This so much pleased her that she took him home and placed him at school.[6]

---

5. "Indeed, some of the most honored names in our history were redemptioners, such as Charles Thomson, Secretary of Congress during the Revolution; Matthew Thornton, a signer of the Declaration of Independence, and the parents of Major General Sullivan."—Scharf's History of Maryland, Vol. I, p. 373.
6. Watson's Annals of Philadelphia and Pennsylvania, Vol. I, p. 568.

Old rowhouses in New Castle, Delaware

chapter two

School Career—Dr. Francis Alison—The New London Academy—Becomes a Teacher—Business Pursuits

*T*he name of the lady who thus befriended Charles Thomson is unknown, but her act of kindness changed the whole course of his life. He was also aided in his education by his brother, Alexander, and he soon became a student in the academy of Dr. Francis Alison at New London, Chester County, Pennsylvania. In a spirit of gratitude, Charles afterward presented his brother with a farm in the vicinity of New Castle. When immigrants from the north of Ireland began to settle in Pennsylvania early in the eighteenth century, large tracts were purchased of the Penn family by companies, and the lands were disposed of to the settlers on easy terms. The London Company took up a large area in southern Chester County, from which originated the names of the townships, New London, London Grove, and London Britain. A Presbyterian church was organized in New London Township on March 26, 1768, composed of the Elk River congregation's northern members. The first pastor was Rev. Samuel Gelston, a native of Ireland, who was succeeded in 1736 by Dr. Francis Alison. In his *History of the Presbyterian*

Churches in the United States, Dr. Robert Ellis Thompson[1] describes the character of the early ministers as follows:

> Especially they have served the country as educators of the
> Middle States, and of those which lie west of them. Their early
> ministers were generally graduates of Glasgow, and it was they
> who established the many academies of those States, in which
> young men were given an education which would at least have
> fitted them to enter any American college. This threw the Pres-
> byterian clergy into contact with others than their own people,
> enlarged their influence for good, and caused their church to be
> more highly esteemed. In view of the church requirement that
> none but educated men should be regarded as candidates for the
> ministry, this combination of the schoolmaster with the pastor
> was regarded as natural and proper, as indeed their every semi-
> nary was a seed plot for the ministry. They thus rendered a great
> service in maintaining a high educational standard at a time when
> the poverty of the country, the general indifference to whatever
> was 'unpractical,' and the active hostility of many sects to literary
> culture made this very much harder to do than it is to-day.

Dr. Alison was born in the north of Ireland in 1705 and was educated at the universities of Edinburgh and Glasgow. He came to America
in 1734 and was employed for a time as a tutor in the family of John
Dickinson. He was installed as pastor of the New London Presbyterian
Church in 1736, where he remained for fifteen years. In 1741, he opened
a private academy in New London, one of the earliest in this country.[2]
At this time, the only means of education in the middle colonies was

1. Dr. Thompson is himself a native of Ulster and came to this country in 1857. After graduating from
the University of Pennsylvania, he was admitted to the Presbyterian ministry, and became a professor in the
University. He is at present the President of the Central High School of Philadelphia, one of the largest free
colleges in the world.
2. Historical Discourse Delivered on the Occasion of the One Hundred and Fiftieth Anniversary of the
New London Presbyterian Church, Chester Co., Pa., Jan. 22, 1876; by the Pastor, Rev. Robert P. DuBois.
See also Biographical sketches of the Founder and Principal Alumni of the Log College; edited by A. Alexander, D.D., p. 108.

found in the academies. There were no colleges in New York, New Jersey, Pennsylvania or Maryland, but there were several excellent academies, among them, one on the Neshaminy in charge of Rev. William Tennent, several in Philadelphia, Rev. Samuel Blair's school at Fagg's Manor, West Nottingham Academy in charge of Rev. Samuel Finley, and Dr. Alison's academy at New London.

In 1744, Dr. Alison's school was established permanently by the Synod of Philadelphia, when the following plan was adopted:

1. That all persons who please may send their children and have them instructed *gratis* in the languages, philosophy, and divinity;
2. That the school be supported for the present by yearly contributions from the congregations under their care;
3. That if any funds remain after paying the salaries of the master and tutor, they shall be expended in the purchase of books and other necessaries for the school.

Dr. Alison was appointed principal with a salary of £20 and the privilege of choosing an usher at a salary of £15. In 1748, the salaries were raised to £40 and £20, and to meet this in part, each student, except the needy, was to be assessed twenty shillings a year. The original academy building was located at Thunder Hill, about two miles southwest of the village of New London. John F. Watson and Henry Simpson both located the academy in Maryland, being led into the error on account of the long dispute over the boundary line. Tradition says that the school was first opened in the loft of a spring house that stood on the late John Whitcraft farm, now owned by his grandson, Robert Crowl. Mrs. George Storey, one of the oldest residents of New London, has distinct recollections of this building, the site of which is marked by some garden shrubs.

Pennsylvania owes much to Dr. Alison for his careful training of many young men who became prominent either in the church or in the nation's councils. Among his pupils were Charles Thomson, John

Dickinson, Ebenezer Hazard, Dr. John Ewing, David Ramsay, Thomas McKean, James Smith, and George Read. Dr. Alison instructed at least four governors, eight Congressmen, and four signers of the Declaration of Independence. The President of Yale College declared him "the greatest classical scholar in America," and he was frequently called the "Busby of the Western Hemisphere."[3] He loved the sciences as well as the classics, which may be seen in the following letter to President Ezra Stiles, of Yale, after an unsuccessful effort to discover a comet:

> As I hope with more certainty and less trouble to acquire this kind of knowledge in the next stage of my existence, if it be necessary, I have determined to give myself no farther trouble till I be allowed to converse with Newton, Halley, Whiston, and Flamstead, and some others of the same complexion, if these names be allowed to shine in one great constellation in heaven. Yet I am far from blaming you for your careful and accurate researches; they may make you more useful here and form your taste to examine the works of God with a higher satisfaction in the coming world. [4]

In 1752, Dr. Alison purchased a tract of land in New London village and erected a large brick mansion for the use of the academy; but before it could be occupied, he resigned to accept the rectorship of the Academy of Philadelphia. The New London Academy passed into the hands of Rev. Alexander McDowell, who removed it to Newark, Delaware, where it became the foundation of Delaware College and Academy. The connection between these two institutions is clearly shown in the charter granted to the Newark Academy in 1769 by Thomas and Richard Penn:

---

3. Richard Busby was born in Lincolnshire, England, in 1606. In 1628, he graduated from Oxford, and in 1640, he became headmaster of Westminster school. His reputation as a teacher soon became so great that many of the noblest families entrusted their children to his care. He, himself, once boasted that sixteen of the bishops who then occupied the bench had been birched with his "little rod." Among his students were South, Dryden, Locke, Prior and Bishop Atterbury. He died in 1695, in his ninetieth year.
4. The Life of Ezra Stiles, D.D., LL.D., by Abiel Holmes, A.M., p. 68.

Whereas, the Rev. Messrs. John Thompson, Adam Boyd, Robert Cross, Francis Alison, Alexander McDowell, and some others, about twenty years since, erected a public school in the province of Pennsylvania, for the instruction of youth in the learned languages, mathematics, and other branches of useful literature, and to qualify them for admission into colleges and universities; which school they supported with much care and expense, to the great advantage and benefit of the public: And whereas, the said school, so as aforesaid, originally in the province of Pennsylvania, hath been removed and is now kept in the town of Newark, in the county of Newcastle.

Dr. Alison was elected Vice-Provost of the College of Philadelphia in 1755, a position he held until his death in 1779. In his funeral sermon Dr. Ewing thus referred to him:

All who knew him acknowledge that he was frank, open and ingenuous in his natural temper; warm and zealous in his friend-ship; catholic and enlarged in his sentiments; a friend to civil and religious liberty; abhorring the intolerant spirit of persecution, bigotry, and superstition, together with all the arts of dishonesty and deceit. His humanity and compassion led him to spare no pains nor trouble in relieving and assisting the poor and distressed by his advice and influence, or by his private liberality; and he has left behind him a lasting testimony of the extensive benevolence of his heart in planning, erecting and nursing, with constant attention and tenderness, the charitable scheme of the widows' fund, by which many helpless orphans and destitute widows have been seasonably relieved and supported; and will, we trust, continue to be relieved and supported, so long as the Synod of New York and Philadelphia shall exist.[5]

5. Annals of the American Pulpit by William B. Sprague, Vol. 3, p. 76.

While a student at the New London Academy, Charles Thomson frequently gave manifestations of his ardent zeal for knowledge. On one occasion, he got hold of some loose leaves of the *Spectator*, and admiring its style, he so longed to possess the whole work that he walked all night to Philadelphia and returned the next day in time to be present in his classes. He was charmed with the study of Greek, and he walked to Amboy to visit a British officer there who had the reputation of being a fine Greek scholar. His relatives and friends urged him to commence the study of theology after having finished his academic course. For this purpose, they recommended to him the reading of certain theological works. It is related that he once inquired from whence these writers drew their religious knowledge. His relatives answered: "From the Holy Scriptures, most assuredly," and seemed to be surprised at his asking such a question. "Well, then," replied young Charles, "if they whom you so highly recommend as models drew their religious instruction from the Scriptures, I shall apply directly to the same source, instead of taking knowledge at second hand."[6] Although he had no intention of preparing for the ministry, he at once began a careful study of the Bible and laid the foundations of that intimate knowledge of the Scriptures, which he displayed in later years.

From the most reliable evidence at hand, it appears that Charles Thomson at once became a teacher on leaving the New London Academy. He made his home for a time in the family of John Chambers,[7] who resided on a large farm, on the edge of New Castle County, about one hundred yards from the Pennsylvania line. Thomson opened a subscription school in the cooper shop that stood on the Chambers farm, and Sarah Black Chambers, the chronicler of the family, who died in 1898, at the age of ninety, often remarked that he was considered the best teacher in all that region.

---

6. The Friend: A Religious and Literary Journal, Vol. I, p. 230.
7. John Chambers married Deborah Dobson in the county of York, England, April 13, 1699. They came to Philadelphia with a certificate from Friends in England in 1713, and two years later, they settled along White Clay Creek, in New Castle County, where they took up twelve hundred acres of land, a part of which, has always been known as the "Hopyard." This property has been in the Chambers family for nearly two centuries.

While a student at the New London Academy, Thomson made the acquaintance of Dr. Franklin and frequently sought his advice regarding the prospects of a suitable vocation in Philadelphia. Being President of the Board of Trustees in the new Academy of Philadelphia, Franklin made use of the opportunity to secure Thomson's position in the school.[8] The Trustees of the Academy held a meeting on December 20, 1750, and the minutes contain the following notice concerning Thomson:

> Mr. Charles Thomson having offered himself as a Tutor in
> the Latin and Greek School, and having been examined and
> approved by of by the Rector, is admitted as a Tutor in the Latin
> and Greek School at the rate of sixty pounds a year, to commence
> on the seventh day of January next.

The same day, David James Dove was elected master of the English school. Dove soon resigned from his position and opened a school in Germantown, where he led an erratic career as a teacher.[9] He substituted disgrace for corporal punishment and generally stuck the birch into the back part of the collar of the unfortunate culprit, who was compelled to take his stand upon the platform, with this badge of disgrace towering above his head. He also had a contrivance to secure regular attendance at school. This was to send five or six pupils after the tardy boys, with a bell and lighted lantern, and in this way, they were escorted through the streets to school. Dove happened to be late on a certain morning, and he found himself waited upon in the usual fashion. He submitted to the ordeal, and following the lantern and bell, marched with great solemnity to school, to the gratification of the pupils and entertainment of the spectators.[10]

Thomson began his duties in the academy on January 7th, 1751. His services must have pleased the authorities, for new responsibilities were soon added to his position. On July 14, 1752, the trustees resolved that "Charles Thomson, one of the Tutors in the Latin School, having some

---

8. This institution was founded in 1749, as an academy and charitable school. In 1755, it was chartered as the College, Academy, and Charitable School of Philadelphia, and after a series of troubles during the Revolution, it was finally incorporated in 1791, as the University of Pennsylvania.

9. History of the Germantown Academy by Rev. William Travis, Philadelphia, 1882, p. 17.

10. Memoirs of a Life Chiefly Passed in Pennsylvania by Alexander Graydon, p. 14.

time since, at the request of the trustees, undertaken to collect and keep account of the school money, and having in pursuance thereof gathered in and paid the Treasurer upwards of five hundred pounds, be allowed two pounds, ten shillings percent, on money by him so collected and paid."

Thomson remained as a teacher in the academy until July 1755. From the meager accounts of the school at that time, it appears that he was a most capable instructor. When he came to Philadelphia, he was regarded as one of the best scholars in the province, especially in the classics. He carried this reputation into the schoolroom and gave to his classes the best results of his training under Dr. Francis Alison. Thomson's resignation is officially noticed in the minutes of the trustees, as follows:

> A letter to the trustees from Mr. Charles Thomson, one of the Tutors in the Latin School, was read acquainting them with his intention of leaving the academy within two or three months, having a design to apply himself to other business. Mr. Peters was, therefore, desired to assist Mr. Alison in providing another in his room. The trustees, at the same time, declared themselves well satisfied that the said Mr. Thomson had discharged the duties of his place with capacity, faithfulness and diligence.

Two years later, Thomson again became a teacher, having been elected to a position in what is now the William Penn Charter School, Philadelphia.[11] The minute books of the Overseers for "the twenty-seventh day of ninth month, 1757," state that Charles Thomson was engaged to take charge of the Latin School, it being "mutually agreed that he shall enter into service next Second Day morning, 29th inst., for one year certain, at the rate of one hundred and fifty pounds per annum, and in case of any dissatisfaction arising on either side, six months' notice to be given before he shall be at liberty to decline the service or we to discharge him."

---

11. This school was established under instructions from Wm. Penn in 1689. It was called at first the "Friends' Public Schools." It received charters from William Penn in 1697, 1701, 1708 and 1711. Among its prominent teachers in early times were George Keith, Thomas Makin, Charles Thomson, Robert Proud and Jeremiah Todd. It is one of the oldest secondary schools in the country. It is at present located on Twelfth street, below Market, and is in a flourishing condition, in charge of Dr. Richard M. Jones, Headmaster.

Thomson was introduced into the Latin School at the appointed time, and his services having proved satisfactory, his salary was increased in 1758 to two hundred pounds per annum. At a meeting of the Overseers, held "2nd of 1st mo., 1760," there is this minute:

Charles Thomson now attending informed the Board that as he intends to enter into other business the next year, he has concluded to resign his place as Master of the Latin School at the expiration of the present year, and pursuant to the terms of our first agreement, he gives this timely notice of his intentions which remains under consideration.

One "6th of 10th mo., 1760," there is this minute:

Charles Thomson attended the Board and made resignation of his charge of the School agreeable to notice formerly given; at same time he laid before the Board a Catalogue of the Library belonging to the Latin School and also, his Account.

Thomson seems to have severed his connection with the School at this time, and after fruitless efforts to find a successor, the Latin School was temporarily given up, until September 5, 1761, when Robert Proud,[12] the historian of Pennsylvania, was elected teacher of the School, and it resumed operations.[13]

---

12. Robert Proud was born in Yorkshire, England, May 10th, 1728. About 1750, he went to London and made his home in a family of Friends. He devoted his leisure time to the study of medicine, but soon became disgusted with it. In 1759, he came to America, and two years later became a teacher, a vocation which he followed until 1790. In 1797, his History of Pennsylvania appeared, in the publication of which he was aided by some of his former pupils. He died a bachelor in 1813.

13. While teaching in this school, Thomson boarded for a time in the house of David J. Dove, his former colleague in the Academy of Philadelphia. He soon found that Dove and his wife were addicted to scandal and gossip, which became disgusting to his honest nature. John F. Watson says: "Wishing to leave them, and still dreading their reproach when he should be gone, he hit upon an expedient to exempt himself. He gravely asked them one evening if his behavior since he had been their boarder had been satisfactory to them. They readily answered, 'O, yes.' 'Would you then be willing to give me a certificate to that effect?' asked Thomson. 'O, certainly,' was the reply. A certificate was given, and the next day he departed from them in peace.

On leaving the Friends' School, Thomson next engaged in mercantile pursuits. For a while, he was an importer, receiving large invoices for dry goods, hats, etc., from various London firms. He was following this business at the time of the passage of the Stamp Act, and in settling his accounts with the foreign houses, he frequently complained of the bad effects of the measure upon trade.[14] At the same time, he was also concerned in the Batsto Furnace, near the junction of the Batsto and Egg Harbor rivers, New Jersey. This furnace was built in 1766 by Charles Read. It is mentioned in the Journals of the Continental Congress as "Dr. Coxe's ironworks in the Jerseys." During the Revolution, it was employed in casting cannon-shot and bombshells for the American army, and it remained in operation until after the middle of this century.[15] Thomson was successful in his business enterprises and had considerable wealth when he became Secretary of Congress. As early as 1760, he subscribed liberally for the paving of Second Street, between Market and Race, it being the first regularly paved street in the city.[16] Although his fortune was considerably impaired during the Revolution on account of his close application to public affairs, he was able, in 1780, to take stock to the amount of $15,000 in the new Pennsylvania Bank.

14. Collections of the New York Historical Society for the year 1878, p. 5.

15. A Concise History of the Iron Manufacture of the American Colonies by J. B. Pearse, p. 54; also History of American Manufactures by J. L. Bishop, Vol. I, p. 549; also, History of the Manufacture of Iron in All Ages by J. M. Swank, p. 120.

16. This street used to be very muddy, and one of the Whartons getting mired there, between Chestnut and High streets, was thrown from his horse, and had his leg broken.

Dr. Francis Alison

Benjamin Franklin drawing electricity from the sky by
Benjamin West.

William Penn Charter School

Batsto Manor House

chapter three

Charles Thomson, "The Man of Truth" — Interest in Indian Affairs — Thomson's Enquiry

As early as 1755, Thomson became a man of great influence throughout the province of Pennsylvania, and he began to display that character which he maintained throughout his life; so that, according to Dr. Ashbel Green, it was a popular mode of affirming the truth of anything to say, "It is as true as if Charles Thomson's name were to it." For several years, the colony's frontier inhabitants were held in a state of terror on account of the Indian outrages. In 1686 William Penn bought of the Indians a tract of land lying between the Delaware River and Neshaminy Creek and extending northwestwardly as far as a man could ride on horseback in two days. This agreement was not carried out until 1737, when the proprietaries and the Indians met at Easton on August 25th to make a treaty. It was finally decided that the purchase of 1686 be consummated by commencing at Wrightstown, in Bucks County, and terminating at a spot that a man could reach in one and a half days' walk.

Edward Marshall, one of the walkers, started from Wrightstown at sunrise on September 19, 1737, and at noon the next day, he had reached the Tobyhanna Creek, beyond the Endless Mountains. A line was drawn from this point to the Delaware River; the Indians were under the impression that it would extend to the river's nearest point. But the surveyors drew a rectangular line, terminating at the mouth of the Lackawaxen, thus robbing the Indians of their favorite hunting grounds on the Minisink. Great dissatisfaction followed, ending in open warfare upon the whites in 1755. Within a few years, the Indian tribes became desirous of peace, and arrangements were made for a treaty at Easton in August 1757.[1] The agents representing the Province of Pennsylvania were Messrs. Norris, Fox, Hughes, Roberdeau, Galloway, and Strickland with Conrad Weiser, the interpreter. The Indians came to the number of three hundred, representing ten tribes, and Tedyuscung,[2] a chief of the Delawares, was appointed to speak for them at the conference.

The Friendly Association, organized by several prominent Quakers in 1756, greatly influenced this treaty's negotiations. The purposes of this body are set forth by Gough in his *History of the People Called Quakers*, as follows:

> The Friendly Association was first promoted in the 11th month, 1756, and continued to the 19th of the 4th month, 1763; during which time committees were annually elected by the subscribers, who met on the 19th of the 4th month in each year, to receive

---

1. "Easton was a favorite place for holding councils with the Indian chiefs between the years 1754 and 1761, while the French were endeavoring to seduce the tribes on the Susquehanna and Ohio from their allegiance to the English. It was not uncommon to see from 200 to 400 Indians present on these occasions, and many of the dignitaries of the province and of other colonies."—Day's Historical Collections of Pennsylvania. At Easton two treaties had been held in the preceding year, 1756. One of them in July by Governor Morris, and the other in November by Governor Denny, when some captives were brought in and restored to their connections. These treaties appear to have been promoted by a conference between some of the Quakers in Philadelphia and a few Indians who had visited the city.

2. "A Delaware chief settled at Wyoming in 1758, at the public expense intending thereby to place him and his people as a frontier defense. They sent on a force of fifty men, as carpenters, masons and laborers, who erected ten or twelve houses, of fourteen by twenty feet, and one for himself, of sixteen by twenty-four feet. He was an artful, wily chief, of more than common selfishness and intrigue for an Indian, and withal was intemperate and aspiring."—Watson's Annals of Philadelphia and Pennsylvania, Vol. 2, p. 127.

from the said committee an account of their transactions, and
expenditure of the money raised, which amounted to £4004,
1*s., 6d.,* which was chiefly laid out in presents to the Indians and
delivered to them at the public treaties either by the Governors
of the Province, Morris and Denny, on behalf of the subscribers,
or by the permission or knowledge of the said Governors, as well
as to conciliate the minds of the Indians as to encourage them to
seek out and release the captives remaining among them. £430 of
the above sum was contributed by the Mennonites, who intrusted
it to the care of the said association, and besides the above
contributions, the sum of £236, 14s. was raised by a number of
religious Germans, called Schwenkfelders, which they directed to
be applied for the particular purpose of the redemption of captives.

The Friendly Association desired to send representatives to the conference at Easton, but the governor denied their request. Some of the
association's leading members then prompted Tedyuscung to demand a
secretary of his choosing to take the minutes of the treaty. The governor
was compelled to accede to the demand on the threat of the Indian chief
to retire from the conference. Charles Thomson, of Philadelphia, was at
once appointed secretary. He soon won the confidence of the Indians by
his truthfulness and efforts to secure justice for the various tribes. In the
treaty of the preceding year, Tedyuscung delivered an eloquent oration
on the wrongs of his nation; but those parts of his speech, which reflected
on the conduct of the provincial government, were omitted in the official
reports. Thomson determined to prevent any intrigues against the Indians, and he labored to have the whole truth appear in the proceedings
of the treaty. That the provincial agents had planned certain intrigues
is evident from Thomson's letter to Mr. Samuel Rhoads, dated July 28,
1757. He said:

> I need not mention the importance of the business we are come
> about. The welfare of the province and the lives of thousands
> depend upon it. That an affair of so much weight should be

managed with soberness all will allow. How then must it shock
you to hear that pains seem to have been taken to make the King
drunk every night since the business began. The first two or
three days were spent in deliberating whether the King should be
allowed the privilege of a clerk. When he was resolute in asserting
his right and would enter on no business without having a secretary of his own, they at last gave it up, and seem to have fallen on
another scheme, which is to unfit him to say anything worthy of
being minuted by his own secretary. On Saturday, under pretense
of rejoicing for the victory gained by the King of Prussia, and
the arrival of the fleet, a bonfire was ordered to be made and
liquor given to the Indians to induce them to dance. For fear they
should get sober on Sunday and be fit next day to enter on business, under pretense that the Mohawks had requested it, another
bonfire was ordered to be made and more liquor given them.

On reaching Easton, Thomson discovered that the governor had
neglected to send certain important deeds, and he at once wrote to that
official as follows:

May it please your Honor:

I think it my duty to inform you, that before I knew of any
intention of my being nominated by Tedyuscung to take the
minutes of the Treaty with him and the Indians now in this town,
I spent some time in reading some of the former Indian treaties
and made extracts from several of them, and observed that in the
treaty of 1728, there is entered a deed from the Indians dated
in 1718, reciting the several former deeds and bargains of sale
of lands made by the Indians; that in the said treaty of 1728,
this deed was acknowledged and ratified by the Indians, and
the boundaries ascertained more accurately than before. And
on examining, this morning, the several deeds delivered by your
Honor's orders to be read to the Indians, and entered on the

minutes of the present treaty, I find the said deed of 1718 is not among them, and having a printed copy of the said deed and treaty in my custody, I could not, consistent with my duty under my present circumstances, nor the concern I have for the honor of his majesty, King George, and the real interest of this Province, omit thus submitting the premises to your Honor's consideration.

I am, may it please your Honor,
Your most obedient servant,
Easton, August 4, 1757
Charles Thomson

The Indians contended that the Six Nations had no right to sell lands to the English, but after copies of all the deeds had been made and given to them, they signed a peace treaty and became the allies of the English in the wars against the French.

Two subsequent treaties were held at Easton in 1758, at the last of which a general peace was settled for Pennsylvania and all the other provinces. All disputes over land claims were, by mutual consent, referred to the King of England. At one of these treaties, Thomson was adopted into the tribe of the Delawares and given the name "Wegh-wu-law-mo-end,"—"The man who tells the truth." From this time, his name was regarded as an emblem of truth, and in all the factional disputes of the Revolutionary period, his judgment was respected.[3] When a Congressional paper appeared containing his signature, the expression was frequently heard, "Here comes the Truth." A gentleman from Albany, visiting Thomson in his old age, inquired what caused such explicit faith to be put in the documents signed by him. The modest reply was, "It was well known that I had resolved in spite of consequences, never to put my official signature to any account, for the accuracy of which I could not vouch as a man of honor."

3. "I do not remember that any representation to which the name of this estimable man was attached, ever proved to be false, or in any material circumstance incorrect."—Life of Ashbel Green, by Rev. J. H. Jones, p. 48.

Thomson's experience as secretary of the treaty at Easton made him the leading authority on all questions relating to the Indians. The extent of his influence is best described in his own language:

> In the year 1757, happening to be present at a treaty held at Easton, in the State of Pennsylvania, with the Indians, who were commonly distinguished by the name of Delawares, for the purpose of making peace, and having by a concurrence of circumstances, gained the confidence of the Indians who came to treat, I was admitted into their council, and obliged to enter deep into their politics and investigate their claims. This led me to inquire touching the state of this nation, and to examine all the treaties and conferences held with them from the first settlement of the province; and having in the year following attended another treaty with the same at which were present the chiefs of the Six Nations, and still retaining the confidence of the Delawares, and being by a solemn act adopted into their nation and called to assist in their councils, I had an opportunity of presenting any inquires, and gaining some knowledge of their internal policy, customs, and manners.[4]

In 1758, Thomson was commissioned by the provincial authorities to examine the cause of the Indian troubles in the Wyoming Valley. Proceeding to Fort Allen, he learned that two hundred of the Six Nations had set out with a resolution to go to war against the English. In making his official report to Governor Denny, Thomson wrote:

> From further enquiry among the Indians, we had some intimation that the Seneka nation were in general dissatisfied with the Government for something that happened in a Treaty with Sir William Johnson. Soon after Sir William received the commission to negotiate Indian affairs, he called a council of all the nations. To

---

4. Collections of the Historical Society of Pennsylvania, Vol. I, p. 80.

this a great number came. He told them that the King had at several times sent out large presents to the Indians of which they had been cheated by the Governments to which they were sent, but that it should not be so any more, that he was the only man who had power to treat with the Indians, and that he would see them righted. This, as it awakened the jealousy of the Indians, raised in them a disrespect for the other Governments, as they imagined they had no authority to treat, and that councils or treaties held with them were of no significance. Besides, a report was very generally propagated among the Senekas, but by whom uncertain, that the King had sent large presents for the Indians of Pennsylvania, which the government of Pennsylvania had appropriated to their own use; and as the road of communication between the government and the Senekas has been for some time shut, and no free intercourse between them and us, no means were used to remove this groundless report till it became universally believed, and the nation in general exasperated against the Pennsylvanians; and this was thought to be one reason that the chief man, though more inclined to the English than the French, and though he has kept himself and his town quiet, yet has used little care to restrain those who had any inclination to go to war with us.[5]

In 1759, Thomson published a book entitled, *An Enquiry into the Causes of the Alienation of the Delaware and Shawenese Indians from the British Interest.* In preparing this work, he made a careful study of all the Indian treaties and deeds. It contains an interesting account of the relations between the various tribes and the English. In the introduction, he speaks as follows concerning the alienation of the Indians from the British interests:

It has been to many a Cause of Wonder, how it comes to pass that the English have so few Indians in their Interest, while the

---

5. Pennsylvania Archives, from 1756-1760, Vol. 3, p. 418.

French have so many at Command; and by what Means, and for what Reasons those neighboring Tribes in particular, who, at the first Arrival of the English in Pennsylvania, and for a long Series of Years afterwards, shewed every Mark of Affection and Kindness, should become our most bitter Enemies, and treat those whom they so often declared they looked upon as their Brethren, nay as their own Flesh and Blood, with such barbarous Cruelties.

By some they are looked on as faithless and perfidious; while others, considering their former Friendship, the many Services they have done the English, and the steady Attachment they have showed to our Interest during several Wars with France, imagine there must be some Cause for this Change in their Behavior. The Indians themselves, when called upon in a public Treaty, to explain the Motives of their Conduct, declare that the Solicitations of the French, joined with the Abuses they have suffered from the English, particularly in being cheated and defrauded of their Land, have at length induced them to become our Enemies and to make War upon us.

Thomson's *Enquiry* also throws considerable light on the Walking Purchase of 1737, quoting the following interesting affidavit made by Joseph Knowles:

June 30th, 1757, I, Joseph Knowles, living with Timothy Smith at the Time of the Day and half's Walk with the Indians (Timothy Smith then Sheriff from Buck's County) do say, that I went some Time before to carry the Chain, and help to clear a Road, as directed by my Uncle Timothy Smith. When the Walk was performed, I was then present, and carried Provisions, Liquors, and Bedding. About Sun-rising we set out from John Chapman's Corner at Wright's-town and travelled until we came to the Forks of Delaware, as near as I can remember was about one of the Clock the same Day. The Indians then began to look sullen and murmured that the Men walked so fast and several Times that

Afternoon called out, and said to them, you run; that's not fair,
you was to walk. The Men appointed to walk paid no Regard to
the Indians but were urged by Timothy Smith and the rest of the
Proprietor's Party, to proceed until the Sun was down. We were
near the Indian Town in the Forks: The Indians denied us going
to the Town on Excuse of a Cantico. We lodged in the Woods
that Night. Next Morning, being dull rainy Weather, we set out
by the Watches, and two of the three Indians, that walked the
Day before, came and travelled with us about two or three Miles,
and then left us, being very much dissatisfied, and we proceeded
by the Watches until Noon. The above I am willing to qualify
to [i.e., make affidavit to] any Time when desired. Witness my
Hand the Day and Year above said. —Jos. Knowles.

The author then modestly describes the circumstances leading to his
appointment as secretary of the treaty of 1757:

Before the public business began, Tedyuscung applied to the
Governor to allow him the liberty of appointing a Person to
take down the minutes of the Treaty for him with the Secretary
appointed by the Governor. He had seen the Secretary of the
Province, at the last Easton treaty, throw down his Pen, and
declare he would not take Minutes when Complaints were made
against the Proprietors. He did not know but the same Thing
might happen again, as the same Complaints would be repeated.
Besides, the Business to be transacted was of the utmost importance, and required to be exactly Minuted, which he thought
might be best done by the Method he proposed. The Governor
then presented George Croghan to Tedyuscung, and the Day
following told him, that Sir William Johnson had constituted and
appointed Mr. Croghan his Deputy-Agent for Indian Affairs in
this Province, with particular Directions to hear any Complaints,
and assist in accommodating the Differences the Indians might
have with his Majesty's Subjects, and particularly those set forth

at the Treaty in November last. As to the Matter of a Secretary, he let Tedyuscung know that, by a particular Agreement, between him and Mr. Croghan at the last Treaty at Lancaster, no one was to take Minutes of the Proceedings but the Secretary appointed by Mr. Croghan; that he had been farther told, it was the constant Practice of Sir William Johnson, as well as all others who have the Conduct of Indian Affairs, to employ their own Secretaries. 'And as this Method,' continues he, 'was settled at Lancaster as a Precedent to be observed in future Treaties, I shall not take upon me to make any alteration in this Respect.'

Tedyuscung looking upon this as a Denial, was much dissatisfied. The Refusal of a Demand so just and reasonable, and which he had made only for the sake of Truth and Regularity, awakened his Suspicion and induced him to believe that there was a Design to lead him on blindfold, and in the Dark, or to take advantage of his Ignorance. Wherefore, considering the Demand he made no longer as a Matter of Favour, but what he had a right to, and not only as reasonable, but absolutely necessary to come at the Truth; and as it had been a Thing agreed upon in his Council at home he resolved once more to insist on its being granted, and if the Governor persisted in refusing it to him, he determined not to treat, but to break up and go home. This being made known to the Governor, he told Tedyuscung, that as no Indian chief before him ever demanded to have a Clerk, and none had ever been appointed for Indians in former Treaties, nay as he had not even nominated one on the part of the Province, he could not help declaring it against his judgment. 'However, to give you a fresh Proof of my Friendship and Regard, if you insist upon having a Clerk, I shall no longer oppose it.'

Four days being spent in this Debate, the public Treaty began the next Day, Tedyuscung having first nominated a Person to take Minutes of the Proceedings for him. The Person nominated was one Charles Thomson, who had at the particular Request of Mr. Peters, taken Minutes at the last Easton Treaty, and of whom it is likely that the Indians had conceived a good Opinion from the close Attention he gave to the Business, when the Secretary of the Province seemed confused and threw down his Pen.[6]

In closing the *Enquiry*, Thomson says:

> Here then, the Affair rests. If the proper Papers, and true State of the Case be laid before the King and Council for a just Determination; if the Indians be assisted in making this Settlement, secured in their Property, and instructed in Religion and the civil Arts, agreeable to their Request, and the Trade with them regulated and set on such a Footing that they may be secure from Abuse, there is not the least Doubt but the Alliance and Friendship of the Indians may be forever secured to the British Interest; but should these Things be neglected, the Arms of the French are open to receive them.
>
> We have already experienced the Cruelties of an Indian War, and there are more Instances than one to show they are capable of being our most useful Friends or most dangerous Enemies. And whether, for the future, they are to be the one or the other, seems now to be in our own Power. How long Matters will rest so, or whether, if the present Opportunity be neglected, such another will ever return, is altogether uncertain. It becomes Men of Wisdom and Prudence to leave nothing to Chance where Reason can decide.

Thus, ends Thomson's *Enquiry*, a work of which Justin Winsor wrote: "We possess in Charles Thomson's *Enquiry* a dispassionate contemporary account of the colonial tergiversations which had provoked these tribes. The friends of colonial honor cannot to-day read it with complacency, nor without a measure of sympathy for Tedyuscung, the chieftain, who was endeavoring to right the native wrongs."[7]

---

6. Thomson's Enquiry, etc., p. 110.
7. The Struggle in America Between England and France, p. 341.

Chief Tedyuscung

The Walking Purchase of 1737

chapter four

Charles Thomson,
"The Sam Adams of Philadelphia"

—His course had been
On those high places, where the dazzling ray
Of honor shines, —and when men's souls were tried
As in a furnace, his came forth like gold.

In describing the causes of the Protestant emigration from Ireland in the eighteenth century, James Anthony Froude says, "The resentment which they carried with them continued to burn in their new homes; and, in the war of Independence, England had no fiercer enemies than the grandsons and great-grandsons of the Presbyterians who had held Ulster against Tyrconnel."[1]

The historian John Adolphus emphasizes this view, claiming that the Presbyterians made the first serious effort towards a union of interests in the colonies. In 1764, when a spirit of discontent began to prevail, the convention of ministers and elders at Philadelphia enclosed a circular letter to all the Presbyterian congregations in Pennsylvania, recommending a general union.[2] As a result of the letter, a union of those congregations immediately took place, while a like course was pursued in all the

---

1. The English in Ireland in the Eighteenth Century, Vol. I, p. 392.
2. Adolphus' History of England, Vol. I, p. 176; see also Smyth's Ecclesiastical Republicanism, and Davidson's History of the Presbyterian Church in Kentucky.

southern provinces. Within a year, the annual Synod at Philadelphia was established, composed of delegates from all the Presbyterian congregations in the colonies. The Congregational churches in New England soon united with the Presbyterian interest, and permanent committees of correspondence were appointed, with the power to consult on political and religious affairs. Adolphus says:

> By this union, a party was prepared to display their power by resistance, and the stamp law presented itself as a favorable object of hostility. Yet, sensible of their own incompetency to act effectually without assistance, and apprehensive of counteraction from the members of the Church of England, and those dissenters who were opposed to violence, they strove with the utmost assiduity to make friends and converts among the disaffected of every denomination.[3]

In reviewing the work of the Presbyterian Church on behalf of civil and religious liberty, the late Dr. Benjamin Holt Rice of Virginia wrote:

> The constitution of the Presbyterian Church is fundamentally and decidedly republican; and it is in a very happy measure adapted to that particular modification of republican institutions, which prevails in the United States. This is too plain to require demonstration; the slightest attention being sufficient to convince anyone that our ecclesiastical constitution establishes in the Church representative government. Hence, the more decidedly a man is a Presbyterian, the more decidedly is he a republican.

Charles Thomson was an elder in the First Presbyterian Church, Philadelphia, when these steps toward union were in progress. The passage of the Stamp Act brought him into the arena of politics, and he threw his whole soul into the cause of the colonists, laboring with so intense

---

3. Adolphus' History of England, Vol. I, p. 177.

a zeal that he became known as "The Sam Adams of Philadelphia."[4] His interest in politics began with his residence in the city. In 1750, he assisted in organizing a society modeled after that of the famous Junta, to which Franklin had belonged in which it was the custom to discuss political questions, while the members were constantly on the alert to assist their fellow citizens. This society was still in existence in 1768 when an effort was made to enlarge its plan. The same year, Thomson wrote to Franklin, "We have established a correspondence in most of the colonies on the continent and in some of the islands and have formed a set of rules or laws for our government which I shall transmit to you by the next opportunity."

On the passage of the Stamp Act, Thomson did not lose hope in the triumph of the American cause. Franklin wrote to him from London in July 1765, "We might as well have hindered the sun's setting. That we could not do. But since it is down, my friend, and it may be long before it rises again, let us make as good a night of it as we can. We may still light candles. Frugality and industry will go a great way toward indemnifying us. Idleness and pride tax with a heavier hand than Kings and Parliaments. If we can get rid of the former, we may easily bear the latter."

He replied as follows: "Be assured the Americans will light lamps of a different sort from those you contemplate."

Thomson took an active interest in preventing John Hughes, the new stamp collector, from entering upon his duties in Philadelphia. He was present at a meeting of the citizens assembled at the State House on October 5, 1765, and was appointed on a committee with James Tilghman, Robert Morris, Archibald McCall, John Cox, William Richards, and William Bradford to demand Hughes' resignation. The committee called upon Hughes about three o'clock in the afternoon, while he was lying sick in bed, and obtained from him a pledge that he would not attempt to perform the functions of his office. The next day Hughes

---

4. "Walked a little about town; visited the market, the State House, the Carpenters' Hall, where the Congress is to sit; then called at Mr. Mifflin's, a grand, spacious and elegant house. Here we had much conversation with Charles Thomson, who is, it seems, about marrying a lady, a relation of Mr. Dickinson's, with five thousand pounds sterling. This Charles Thomson is the Sam Adams of Philadelphia, the life of the cause of liberty, they say."—The Life and Works of John Adams, Vol. 2, p. 358.

THE LIFE OF CHARLES THOMSON

sent for Thomson and asked him if the committee were sincere the day before. Thomson said he was sincere and could only answer for himself. Hughes then exclaimed, "Well, gentlemen, you must look to yourselves; for this is a high affair."

Thus, Thomson made answer, "I do not know, but I hope it will not be deemed rebellion. I know not how it may end, for we have not yet determined whether we will ever suffer the act to take place here or not;" and took his leave.[5] The whole committee called again on Monday and received from Hughes his resignation. The unfortunate stamp agent wrote a lengthy account of his troubles to the commissioners, in which he blamed the Presbyterians and the proprietary party.

Thomson's letters at this time give an excellent account of the excitement prevailing in the colonies as a result of the Stamp Act. On November 9, 1765, he wrote to Messrs. Cook, Lawrence, and Co.:

> The confusion in our city and province, and indeed through the whole colonies, is unspeakable by reason of the late Stamp Act. The courts of justice and the offices of government are all shut; numbers of people who are indebted take advantage of the times to refuse payment and are moving off with all their effects out of the reach of their creditors. Our ports are shut, except to such vessels as were cleared before the 1st inst. Thus, credit is gone, trade and commerce at a stand. That peace which we ardently wished by one fatal act only presents us with a prospect of confusion and beggary.[6]

To Franklin, he wrote November 26, 1769, commenting on England's policy of taxation:

> How much farther they may proceed is uncertain, but from what they have already done, the colonies see that their property is precarious and their liberty insecure. It is true the impositions

5. Goodloe's Birth of the Republic, p. 45.
6. Collections of the New York Historical Society for the Year 1878, p. 15.

already laid are not very grievous; but if the principle is established, and the authority by which they are laid admitted, there
is no security for what remains. The very nature of freedom supposes that no tax can be levied on a people without their consent
given personally or by their representatives. It was not on account
of the largeness of the sum demanded by Charles I. that ship
money was so odious to the commons of England. But because
the principle upon which it was demanded left them nothing,
they could call their own. The continuation of this claim of the
Parliament will certainly be productive of ill consequences, as
it will tend to alienate the affections of the colonies from the
mother country—already it has awakened a spirit of enquiry.
The people by examining have gained a fuller knowledge of their
rights and are become more attentive and watchful against the
encroachments of power, at the same time they are become more
sensible of the resources they have among them for supplying
their real wants. Resentment as well as necessity will drive them
to improve them to the utmost, and from the genius of the
people and the fertility of the soil, it is easy to foresee that in the
course of a few years they will find at home an ample supply of all
their wants. In the meanwhile their strength, power, and numbers
are daily increasing, and as the property of land is parcelled out
among the inhabitants and almost every farmer is a freeholder,
the spirit of liberty will be kept awake and the love of freedom
deeply rooted; and when strength and liberty combine it is easy
to foresee that a people will not long submit to arbitrary sway.[7]

The attitude of the colonies toward the tax on tea gave great of-
fense to the King. The wrath of Parliament was first poured out upon
Massachusetts, and the act closing the port of Boston kindled a flame
of opposition over all the land. On May 13, 1774, the citizens of Boston resolved "that if the other colonies would unite with them to stop

---

7. Ibid., p. 24.

all importations from Great Britain and the West Indies until that act should be repealed, it would prove the salvation of North America and her liberties; but should they continue their exports and imports, there was reason to fear that fraud, power, and the most odious oppression would triumph over justice, right, social happiness and freedom."[8]

When copies of this resolution reached Virginia, her assembly showed every disposition to assist Massachusetts, and the first of June was set apart for a public fast. But while Virginia and Massachusetts were all aglow with the spirit of resistance in British oppression, what was Pennsylvania's sentiment? Here, as in New York, the General Assembly contained a dominating number of passive friends of the crown. Philadelphia was controlled politically by the Friends, and it was well known that without the aid of the city, the province could not be persuaded to take up Massachusetts's cause. Charles Thomson and a few other patriots, who made up the liberty party in Philadelphia, at once set to revolutionize public opinion. The heroism that they displayed should receive ample recognition in history.

Paul Revere arrived in Philadelphia with a copy of the Boston resolutions on May 19, 1774. He also carried with him private letters addressed to Reed, Mifflin, and Charles Thomson. These letters were read at the Coffee House the same day, and after a hasty conference, it was decided to call a meeting of the principal citizens in the long room of the City Tavern on the evening of the next day, Friday, May 20th. Great anxiety was felt as to the possible results of the meeting. Many citizens wished for a decisive expression of sentiment, while another large party favored more temperate measures. Thus, in the conflict of opinions, the entire plan of the meeting was threatened with defeat. Sydney George Fisher writes:

> The liberty party were in a peculiar position. They had to be very
> shrewd and cautious. They could win applause and distinction

---

8. "The impolicy, injustice, inhumanity, and cruelty of the law exceeded all their powers of expression, and they left it to the just censure of God and the world. Copies of this vote were transmitted to all the colonies; the act of Parliament was printed on paper bordered with black, hawked about the streets as a barbarous, cruel, bloody, and inhuman murder, and in some places burnt with great solemnity."—Adolphus' History of England, Vol. 2, p. 117.

neither by violent action nor by violent speech. They had opportunities neither for 'tea parties' nor orations on the eternal rights
of man. The child of liberty which they were nursing could bear
no noise. If they were to build up their party with recruits from
Quakers, Episcopalians, and Germans, they must move slowly
and with cold and calculating sagacity.[9]

The first great object of Thomson, Reed, and Mifflin was to secure
the co-operation of John Dickinson. He had been regarded as conserva-
tive and in line with the Friends' policy, and yet the other party hoped
for his assistance to carry their measures to success. After the Revolution,
Thomson gave a lengthy account of Dickinson's attitude, in a letter to
William H. Drayton, of South Carolina. It appears that when the news
of the Boston Port Bill reached the country, Dickinson gave it as his
opinion that the time had come to step forward. It was secretly arranged
that he should prepare the people's minds through a series of public letters, but before this could be accomplished, Paul Revere had arrived with
the Boston letter. In describing the plan, Thomson writes:

> As the Quakers, who are principled against war, saw the storm
> gathering, and therefore wished to keep aloof from danger, were
> industriously employed to prevent anything being done which
> might involve Pennsylvania farther in the dispute, and as it was
> apparent that for this purpose their whole force would be col-
> lected at the ensuing meeting, it was necessary to devise means so
> to counteract their designs as to carry the measures proposed and
> yet prevent a disunion, and thus, if possible bring Pennsylvania's
> whole force undivided to make common cause with Boston. The
> line of conduct Mr. D. had lately pursued opened a prospect for
> this. His sentiments were not generally known. The Quakers
> courted and seemed to depend upon him. The other party from
> his past conduct hoped for his assistance but were not sure how

---

9. Pennsylvania: Colony and Commonwealth, p. 299.

far he would go if matters came to extremity, his sentiments on
the present controversy not being generally known. It was therefore agreed that he should attend the meeting, and as it would
be in vain for Philadelphia or even Pennsylvania to enter into the
dispute unless seconded and supported by the other colonies,
the only point to be carried at the ensuing meeting was to return
a friendly and affectionate answer to the people of Boston, to
forward the news of their distress to the southern colonies, and to
consult them and the eastern colonies on the propriety of calling
a congress to consult on measures necessary to be taken. If divisions ran high at the meeting, it was agreed to propose the calling
together the Assembly in order to gain time.[10]

Thomson relates that to accomplish this, it was agreed that one of
Dickinson's friends, a rash man, should urge an immediate declaration
in favor of Boston; and that Dickinson should oppose and press for
moderate measures, which would be adopted. Messrs. Reed, Mifflin, and
Thomson arranged to dine with Dickinson on the day of the meeting,
and after a lengthy conference, the latter decided to be present in the evening. Reed and Mifflin then returned to town, while Thomson remained
to bring Dickinson so that all might not seem to have been together.
William B. Reed writes:

> The meeting was large but was composed of the most heteroge-
> neous materials. The proprietary party had sent its representa-
> tives; —many of the leading men among the Friends, and the
> sons of nearly all the officers of government were present; and
> all awaited with great apparent excitement the opening of the
> meeting.[11]

The proceedings of this meeting are graphically described in the following language:

---

10. Collections of the New York Historical Society for the year 1878, p. 275.
11. Life and Correspondence of Joseph Reed, Vol. I, p. 66.

The letter received from Boston was read, after which Reed addressed the assembly with temper, moderation, but in pathetic terms. Mifflin spoke next and with more warmth and fire. Thomson succeeded, and pressed for an immediate declaration in favor of Boston, and making common cause with her; but being overcome with the heat of the room and fatigue (for he had scarce slept an hour two nights past), he fainted and was carried into an adjoining room. Great clamor was raised against the violence of the measures proposed. Dickinson then addressed the company. In what manner he acquitted himself I cannot say. After he had finished the clamor was renewed; voices were heard in different parts of the room, and all was in confusion; a chairman was called for to moderate the meeting and regulate debates; still the confusion continued. As soon as Thomson recovered, he returned into the room. The tumult and disorder were past description. He had not strength to attempt opposing the gust of passion or to allay the heat by anything he could say. He therefore simply moved a question that an answer should be returned to the letter from Boston; this was put and carried. He then moved for a committee to write the answer; this was agreed to, and two lists were immediately made out and handed to the chair. The clamor was then renewed on which list a vote should be taken. At length it was proposed that both lists should be considered as one and compose the committee. This was agreed to, and the company broke up in tolerable good humor, both thinking they had in part carried their point.[12]

The committee referred to by Thomson met the next day, May 21st. They prepared an answer to the Boston letter and addressed a petition to the Governor, signed by nearly one thousand citizens, requesting him to convene the Assembly. The Governor refused to grant the petition, and Thomson regarded that official's reply as well calculated for the meridian of London. As the first of June approached, the feelings of resentment in

---

12. Collections of the New York Historical Society for the year 1878, p. 277.

Philadelphia against Great Britain became manifest. Christopher Marshall writes:

> This being the day when the cruel act for blocking the harbor
> of Boston took effect, many of the inhabitants of this city, to
> express their sympathy and show their concern for their suffering
> brethren in the common cause of liberty, had their shops shut up,
> their houses kept close from hurry and business; also the ring of
> bells at Christ Church were muffled, and rung a solemn peal at
> intervals, from morning till night; the colors of the vessels in the
> harbor were hoisted half-mast high; the several houses of different
> worship were crowded, where divine service was performed, and
> particular discourses, suitable to the occasion, were preached by F.
> Alison, Duffield, Sprout, and Blair. Sorrow, mixed with indigna-
> tion, seemed pictured in the countenance of the inhabitants, and
> indeed the whole city wore the aspect of deep distress, being a
> melancholy occasion.[13]

The governor's refusal to convene the Assembly gave the patriots a fair
pretext for holding a general meeting of the citizens at the State House.
This gathering was convened on June 18 and was attended by fully eight
thousand people. Dickinson and Willing presided, while Dr. Smith,
Reed, and Thomson were the principal speakers. With so much caution
were the meeting proceedings conducted, the speakers were required to
submit their addresses to the President for revision. A general congress
of the colonies was recommended, a committee of correspondence was
appointed,[14] and measures were taken to relieve the sufferers by the Bos-

13. Passages from the Remembrances of Christopher Marshall, p. 6.

14. "The union, effected among the colonies, by means of corresponding committees, was a death-blow
to the authority of Britain; the Americans were sensible of the advantage, and as soon as the co-operation of
all parts of the continent was ensured, advanced bolder claims, diffused broader principles of government,
and assumed with less disguise, the part and mien of defiance. The references made in their declaration to
the rights of nature, the intimation that like their ancestors, they proceeded before the adoption of other
measures, to state their grievances and their rights, and their frequent exhortations to arms, all prove that
plans of revolution and resistance were already meditated and digested. Motives of common safety, when
they had once assumed an hostile position, cemented the jarring interests of the colonies, and for the time
subdued their inveterate jealousies."—Adolphus' History of England, Vol. 2, p. 145.

ton Port Bill. The committee of correspondence issued a call for a general convention at Philadelphia on July 15th and requested the Governor to summon the Assembly members to meet on the first of August. In the meantime, the Governor had been compelled to convene the Assembly on the rumor of Indian hostilities; nevertheless, the convention met at the appointed time and chose Mr. Willing for chairman and Charles Thomson secretary. Resolutions were adopted declaring: that they owed allegiance to George the Third; that unconstitutional independence from the parent state was abhorrent to their principles; that they desired the restoration of harmony with the mother country, on the principles of the constitution; that the inhabitants of the colonies were entitled to the same rights and liberties within the colonies that subjects born in England were entitled to within that realm; that the late acts of Parliament affecting Massachusetts were unconstitutional; that there was an absolute necessity that a congress of the colonies should be immediately assembled, etc. [15] After these meetings, Thomson, Dickinson, and Mifflin, apparently to take an excursion for pleasure, made a tour of the frontier counties to learn the German districts' political sentiment. The Philadelphia meetings were bold in their attitude towards established power, and one writer claims that they became the precedent for the first Jacobin clubs in Paris. In 1822, Thomas Jefferson, writing to Morse, referred to the Philadelphia meeting of June 18th, as follows: "This perilous engine became necessary to precede the Revolution, but I regard it as a collateral power which no man could wish to see in use again."[16]

On October 3, 1774, Thomson was elected as a member of the Pennsylvania Assembly. In this body, he displayed the same shrewdness that had marked his conduct in the town meeting and as a member of

---

15. See the Resolutions in Niles' Principles and Acts of the Revolution, p. 204.

16. The events of 1774-75 are vividly described by Thomson in a letter to Hon. William H. Drayton, of South Carolina, who was preparing a History of the Revolution in the Southern Colonies. Drayton was a member of Congress in 1778, but died in 1779, before his history was completed. After his death, many of his papers were destroyed; but the letter from Thomson escaped, and it was afterwards published in the Pennsylvania Magazine of History and Biography, Vol. 2; also in Collections of the New York Historical Society for the Year 1878. Considerable light is thrown on the same period in Thomson's letter to Dr. David Ramsay, November 4, 1786, published in the Collections of the New York Historical Society for 1878, p. 215.

the committee of correspondence. Here he labored zealously with the other patriots to adopt measures for the common defense. It was necessary to obtain the concurrence of the Germans, upon whom the Liberty party placed great reliance in time of danger. On the other hand, the overzealous had to be restrained to save the Province from being rent to pieces by hostile factions. Immediately after Congress had recommended the formation of State governments, the Whigs held a town meeting in Philadelphia and resolved:

> That the present assembly not having been elected for the purpose of forming a new government, could not proceed therein, without assuming arbitrary power: That a protest be immediately entered by the people of the city and county of Philadelphia against the power of the house to carry into execution the resolve of Congress: That a provincial assembly, elected by the people, be chosen for that purpose: That the present government of the province was not competent to the exigencies of its affairs; and that the meeting would abide by these resolutions, be the consequences what they might.

Charles Thomson and Dickinson opposed this resolution and adhered to the opinion that Pennsylvania's charter institutions could be maintained, even amid revolution.[17] Thomson defended his position in the following able argument:

> The original Constitution of Pennsylvania was very favorable and well-adapted to the present emergencies.

---

17. "Pennsylvania was fairly alive with the idea of independence. Nowhere had the question been more thoroughly discussed than in its press; and nowhere was the opposition to it more strongly intrenched, for it had on its side the proprietary government. Tories could point to the instructions of the Assembly against it as the voice of an eighth of the inhabitants of America. Then, too, warm advocates of independence—Charles Thomson, for instance—desired to retain the charter; agreeing with the Tories, the majority of the Quakers and the proprietary party. Hence it is not easy to describe the political feeling with precision."—Frothingham's Rise of the Republic of the United States, p. 519. Webster, in his History of the Presbyterian Church in America, claims that the Presbyterians generally opposed the throwing off the Proprietary government. Dr. Francis Alison was quite active in this direction, and, as a reward for his services, Richard Penn gave him a tract of fifteen hundred acres at the confluence of the Bald Eagle with the West Branch of the Susquehanna.

The Assembly was annual. The election was fixed to a certain day, on which the freeman who were worth fifty pounds met, or had a right to meet, without summons at their respective county town, and by ballot choose not only Representative for Assembly, but also Sheriff, Coroner, Commissioners for managing the affairs of the County, and Assessors to rate the tax imposed by law upon the estates, real and personal, of the several inhabitants of their county. The members of the House of Assembly when chosen, met according to law on a certain day and chose their Speaker, Provincial Treasurer, and sundry other officers. The House sat on its own adjournment, nor was it in the power of the Governor to prorogue or dissolve it. Hence it is apparent that Pennsylvania had a great advantage over the other colonies, which by being deprived by their Governors of their legal Assemblies or House of Representatives constitutionally chosen were forced into conventions.

The Assembly of Pennsylvania, if they could be brought to take a part, supplied the place of a Convention, with this advantage, that being a part of the Legislature, they preserved the legal forms of government, consequently had more weight and authority among the people. No man could refuse upon himself the consequences of what might follow by his not attended, and the men of his choice were not elected, he had no right to complain, as the majority of the votes decided. The cause of America was every day gaining ground, and the people were growing more and more determined. The timid were acquiring courage, and the wavering confirmed in the opposition. Hence, it was apparent the election would soon be wholly in the power of the Patriot and Whig party. For these reasons, the Whigs who were then members wished to temporize and make use of the Assembly rather than a Convention, but unhappily for the Province, they were thwarted in their measures by a body of men from whom they expected to derive the firmest support.[18]

18. Collections of the New York Historical Society for the Year 1878, p. 282.

Thomson gave freely of his time for the cause of independence and subscribed of his means. At a critical point of the Revolution, when there was great danger of the American army's dissolution for want of provisions, he was one of the patriotic gentlemen who gave their bonds to the amount of $1,300,000, his own subscription being $15,000. While the amount of the bonds was never called for, it is well to hold in remembrance the names of those who came forward and pledged their all to the cause of liberty in time of great peril.

Illustration of the First Presbyterian Church in Philadelphia, Pennsylvania (High Street)

Paul Revere

City Tavern in Philadelphia

Mr. and Mrs. Thomas Mifflin

William Henry Drayton

John Dickinson

chapter five

Secretary of the Continental Congress

"When Heav'n propitious smiled upon our arms,
Or scenes adverse spread terror and alarms,
Trough every change, the patriot was the same –
And FAITH and HOPE attended THOMSON'S name."

— *Gazette of the United States*, July 25, 1789.

*T*he colonists' cause had steadily advanced during the summer of 1774, and on October 5 of that year, the First Continental Congress assembled at Philadelphia. Thomson's active services at the head of the liberty party naturally led to his selection as Secretary of this Congress. In the official Journal of Congress, we find this record:

Monday, September 5, 1774.
 The Congress proceeded to the choice of a President, when the Hon. Peyton Randolph was unanimously elected.[1]
 Mr. Charles Thomson was unanimously chosen Secretary.

Mr. Lynch proposed that Thomson should be appointed Secretary, which was done without opposition, although Mr. Duane and Mr. Jay

_____

1. Peyton Randolph, first President of Congress, died in October 1775, at the seat of Henry Hill, Roxborough, where he had accepted an invitation to dine with other company. He fell from his seat in an apoplectic fit and immediately expired.

were at first inclined to elect a man from their own body. The manner of Thomson's appointment is interesting. He had wed Hannah Harrison on Thursday, September 1st, and coming to Philadelphia in his carriage with his wife on the following Monday, he had alighted when a message came to him from the President of Congress that he must see him immediately. Thomson went and was told that they wished him to take their minutes. He began the duty as a temporary affair, but the service continued throughout the Revolutionary period.[2] On one occasion, Thomson gave the following explanation regarding the matter:

> I was married to my second wife on a Thursday; on the next Monday, I came to town to pay my respects to my wife's aunt and the family. Just as I alighted in Chestnut Street, the doorkeeper of Congress (then first met) accosted me with a message from them requesting my presence. Surprised at this, and not able to divine why I was wanted, I, however, bade my servant put up the horses, and followed the messenger myself to the Carpenters' Hall, and entered Congress. Here was indeed an august assembly, and deep thought and solemn anxiety were observable on their countenances. I walked up the aisle, and standing opposite to the President, I bowed and told him I waited his pleasure. He replied, 'Congress desire the favor of you, sir, to take their minutes.' I bowed in acquiescence and took my seat at the desk.

Although Thomson was present at the opening session of Congress, it appears that he did not begin the actual duties of the office until

---

2. "Congress first sat in the building then called Carpenters' Hall, up the court of that name in Chestnut street. On the morning of the day that they first convened, their future secretary, the now venerable Charles Thomson, who resided at that time in the Northern Liberties, and who afterwards so materially assisted to launch or first-rate republic, had that morning rode into the city, and alighted in Chestnut street. He was immediately accosted by a message from Congress, that they desired to speak with him. He followed the messenger, and, entering the building, has described himself as struck with awe, upon viewing the aspects of so many great and good men, impressed with the weight and responsibility of their situation, on the perilous edge of which they were then advancing. He walked up the aisle, and bowing to the President, desired to know their pleasure. 'Congress desires your services, sir, as their secretary.' He took his seat at the desk and never looked back until the vessel was securely anchored in the haven of independence." – "Revolutionary Reminisces of Philadelphia," in Niles' Principles and Acts of the Revolution.

September 10th. Dr. Herbert Friedenwald, who has made a careful study of the records of the Continental Congress, writes:

> Charles Thomson, as is well known, was elected Secretary upon the first day of the meeting of the Congress of 1774, and he retained his office until the end. But although this was the case, the original Journal covering the first five days of the Congress is not in his hand. For some reason, he seems not to have taken up the duties of his office until the 10th of September. Then he examined what had been recorded during his absence, and made sundry additions, corrections, and erasures. The entry of his own election read originally 'Charles Thomson, Secretary.' This he changed to read, as we find it in the printed Journal, 'Mr. Charles Thomson was unanimously elected Secretary,' and the hand is unmistakable.[3]

The character of the First Continental Congress has called forth the admiration of statesmen and historians. William Pitt, in a speech delivered in Parliament, remarked:

> I must declare and avow, that in all my reading and study,—and it has been my favorite study: I have read Thucydides, and have studied and admired the master states of the world, – that for solidity of reasoning, force of sagacity, and wisdom of conclusion, under such a complication of circumstances, no nation or body of men can stand in preference to the General Congress at Philadelphia.

The roll call indicated that, of the fifty-two delegates elected, forty-four were already present, forming a body of representative Americans, which, for dignity of character and for learning, no subsequent legislative body in our country has been able to surpass. In that Congress were

---

3. Annual Report of the American Historical Association for 1896, Vol. 1, p. 110.

assembled such men as John and Samuel Adams, Stephen Hopkins, Roger Sherman, John Sullivan, John Jay, James Duane, Philip and William Livingston, Joseph Galloway, Thomas Mifflin, Caesar Rodney, Thomas McKean, George Read, Samuel Chase, John and Edward Rutledge, Christopher Gadsden, Henry Middleton, Edmund Pendleton, George Washington, and Patrick Henry. "There is in the Congress," wrote John Adams, "a collection of the greatest men upon the continent in point of abilities, virtues, and fortunes."[4] John Trumbull, in his "Elegy on the Times," refers to this assembly in the following lines:

> Now meet the fathers of his western clime,
> Nor names more noble graced the rolls of fame,
> When Spartan firmness braved the wrecks of time,
> Or Rome's bold virtues fanned the heroic flame.
>
> Not deeper thought the immortal sage inspired,
> On Solon's lips when Grecian senates hung;
> Nor manlier eloquence the bosom fired
> When genius thundered from the Athenian tongue.

Thomson was profoundly impressed on assuming his duties in this august body, and he has left several interesting reminiscences of the occasion. After Congress's organization was affected, the question arose whether the method of voting should be by the colonies, by poll, or by interests.[5] All seemed to be impressed by the difficulty of the problem, and a deep silence prevailed. Thomson said:

> None seemed willing to break the eventful silence until a grave-looking member, in a plain dark suit of minister's gray, and unpowdered wig arose. All became fixed in attention on him. As

---

4. "There are some fine fellows come from Virginia, but they are very high. The Bostonians are mere milksops to them. We understand they are the capital men of the colony, both in fortune and understanding." – Remarks of Joseph Reed, in Life and Correspondence, Vol. 1, p. 74.

5. After considerable discussion and debate, it was resolved that each colony should have one equal vote, whatever might be the number of its deputies.

he proceeded, he evinced such unusual force of argument, such
novel and impassioned eloquence as soon electrified the house.
Then the excited inquiry passed from man to man, who is it?
Who is it? The answer from the few who knew him was, it is
Patrick Henry!

It is not my purpose to enter upon a discussion of this Congress's
deliberations, but it may be remarked that the state papers adopted were
in keeping with the high character of the members. The proceedings
of Congress likewise clearly indicate that Thomson's labors in the town
meeting and the committee of correspondence had not been without
good results. He had strived, with the other patriots, to nationalize the
spirit of resistance to British tyranny and to make the cause of Massachusetts common to all the colonies. He must have been gratified at
the unanimity that characterized Congress's actions; for in claiming their
rights as founded on the immutable laws of nature, the representatives
of the colonies were but expressing the views of the committees of correspondence in which Thomson labored with so much zeal. Even the Tory
historian Adolphus was led to express his admiration of the sentiment
that prevailed in Congress.

No longer [he says], did America exhibit the appearance of rival
colonies, piquing themselves on separate rights, and boasting the
relative advantages of different charters, and different constitu-
tions; all such sentiments were buried in oblivion; the same
grievances, although not felt by all, were complained of by all;
and the same remedy, without apparent previous communication,
was generally recurred to, with the only difference of more or less
violence according to the genius of the people, or the temper of
the favorite leaders.[6]

Dr. Friedenwald ably describes Thomson's methods employed in
keeping the records of Congress in his work entitled, *The Journals and*

6. Adolphus' History of England, Vol. 2, p. 129.

Papers of the Continental Congress. Dr. Friedenwald gives an outline of the material contained in the old manuscripts and shows how these papers were first published by authority of Congress.[7] In a letter to Hon. Mellen Chamberlain, December 23, 1884, Theodore F. Dwight, Chief of Bureau of Rolls and Library in the Department of State, Washington, wrote the following account of the Journals:

> As to the several Journals: Charles Thomson, as you know, was the 'perpetual Secretary' of the Continental Congress; and, from all I can gather, he was a man of the strictest probity, and was most conscientious in the discharge of his important trusts. It would be interesting to discover how much influence he exerted in the first councils. I am confident it was considerable. To him we owe the preservation of all the records of the Continental Congress, – not only the Journals, but all those fragments now so precious, *e.g.,* the original motions, the reports of committees, the small odds and ends, which are the small bones of history. They are all in this room, and at my elbow as I write. One of them, for instance, is the original of Lee's motion reproduced, but without proper explanation, by Force, in the *American Archives.* You allude to it.
>
> The Journals of Congress are, with some very few exceptions, entirely in the handwriting of Thomson. He seems to have been present at every session. The series of the archives of the Congress very properly begins with what he termed the 'Rough Journal,' beginning with the proceedings of September 5, 1774, and ended with the entry of March 2, 1789, and was probably written while Congress was sitting, the entries being made directly after each vote was taken. It is contained in thirty-nine small foolscap folio volumes. The second of the series is a fair copy of the 'Rough Journal,' from September 5, 1775, to January 20, 1779, – in ten volumes folio. From this copy, it is stated in a record in the Bureau, 'the Journals were printed; and such portions as

---

7. Annual Report of the American Historical Association, 1896, p. 85.

were deemed secret were marked or crossed by a committee of Congress, – not to be transcribed.' In this he has amplified some entries and given more care to the style and composition of his sentences.

This explanation will account for the 'two Public Journals.' The 'Rough Journal' should be regarded as the standard. No. 3 of the series of archives is the 'Secret Domestic Journal,' comprising entries from May 10, 1775, to October 26, 1787; the fourth number is a Secret Journal, foreign and domestic, comprising entries from October 18, 1780, to March 29, 1786 (the foregoing two numbers form two volumes). No. 5 is in three volumes, and is called 'Secret Journal of Foreign Affairs,' November 29, 1775, to September 16, 1788. No. 6 is in three volumes and is designated 'An Imperfect Secret Journal'; it contains entries made from the *Journal of Congress*, September 17, 1776, to September 16, 1788. No. 7 is a small quarto volume, containing but few entries, called the 'More Secret Journal.' No. 8 is a folio, Secret Journal A, 1776-1783: the contents of this volume appear to be merely minutes of proceedings, which were afterwards entered on the Public Journals.

* * * * * * * * * *

The Journals, it must be remembered, were not the accounts of an individual, but were the accepted records of Congress; that then, as now, each day's proceedings were read to that body before they obtained the authority necessary for their preservation. I dwell upon this in order that you may not attribute the discrepancies between the originals and the printed Journals to the carelessness of a clerk or of the secretary. In my opinion, the responsibility rests with Congress alone.[8]

In his autobiography, John Adams mentions the fact that motions were frequently made in Congress, which are not to be found in the Journals.

---

8. John Adams: The Statesman of the Revolution, with other Essays by Mellen Chamberlain, p. 121.

When motions were made, and debates ensued in a committee
of the whole house [writes Adams], no record was made of them
by the Secretary, unless the motion prevailed and was reported to
Congress, and there adopted. This arrangement was convenient
for the party in opposition to us, who by this means, evaded the
appearance on the Journals of any subject they disliked.

Thomson himself once remarked that he was led to follow this method
by a remark made by Patrick Henry immediately after the organization
of Congress. Henry referred to the difficulties and distress of the times,
comparing the public circumstances to those of a man in deep embarrass-
ment and trouble, who had called his friends together for advice.

One would propose one thing, and another a different one,
whilst perhaps a third would think of something better suited to
his unhappy circumstances, which he would embrace, and think
no more of the rejected schemes with which he would have nothing to do.[9]
   I thought [said Thomson], that this was very good instruction
to me, with respect to the taking of minutes. What Congress
adopted, I committed to writing; with what they rejected, I
had nothing further to do; and even this method led to some
squabbles with the members who were desirous of having their
speeches and resolutions, however, put to rest by the majority,
still preserved upon the minutes.

And so, for fifteen years, Thomson was retained as Secretary of the
Continental Congress, in some respects one of the most remarkable legislative bodies the world has ever seen. During all these years of service,
his relations with the members of the body were of the most agreeable
character. There was but one occasion when any difference existed. On
September 1, 1779, Henry Laurens, the President of Congress, presented

---

9. American Quarterly Review, Vol. 1, p. 30.

a lengthy complaint, charging Thomson with disrespectful behavior toward him. Laurens claimed that Thomson refused to send him copies
of certain resolutions as requested; that he refused to rewrite in a legible
hand the commission of John Adams to the Court of Versailles; that he
refused to give Laurens two copies of the Journal, for his State, etc.[10]
The scene that followed on Thomson's refusal to supply copies of the
Journal must have been an animated one, according to the version given
by Laurens:

> His first answer was – 'I won't' – I replied, you won't, Mr. Thom-
> son, what language is this? I tell you, I want them for my State –
> to which he again answered, 'I won't,' but added, 'till I have given
> every member present one.' Mr. Thomson then descended from
> the platform; I reached out my hand to take another copy; he
> snatched it from me and said, 'You shan't have it.' This repeated
> insult brought instantly to my mind his former conducts, and
> provoked me to say he was a most impudent fellow, that I had a
> good mind to kick him; he turned about, doubled his fist, and
> said, 'You dare not.' When he had humored himself, he returned
> with many spare Journals in his hand and gave me one. I barely
> asked him if he might not as well have done this at first.[11]

On September 6, 1779, Thomson sent Congress a reply to Laurens'
charges. He claimed that Laurens showed a coldness towards him soon
after becoming president and frequently passed the lie. In this letter,
Thomson took occasion to describe Laurens' general conduct as a presid-
ing officer in rather plain language.

> I saw him at the afternoon sessions [wrote Thomson], so far
> unmindful of his station and dignity as to rise and debate ques-
> tions as a delegate, then sit down, and, as President, hear himself
> replied to, and at one time in one of such debates, so far forget

---

10. Potter's American Monthly, Vol. 6, p. 173.
11. Ibid., p. 174.

himself as to answer from the chair an honorable member from North Carolina by singing aloud, 'Poor little Penny, poor little Penny, sing tan-tarra-ra-ra,' and at another time when he was reading a report brought in by an honorable member from Massachusetts Bay, which was under debate, to stop in the middle of a sentence and exclaim, 'Solomon Grundy! Did you ever see such a Solomon Grundy?' which raised such indignation that the honorable member left the room, and soon after, Congress adjourned.[12]

Thomson made a positive denial to the charge of offering insults to Laurens, and he explained his conduct regarding the distribution of the copies of the Journals as follows:

Accordingly, I opened the bundle, and there were several members at the table. I distinguished Mr. Laurens by delivering him one first. When he asked for another, I desired to stay till I had delivered one to each member. When he repeated his demand, he did it in a tone and manner that I confess gave me offence, and at the instant, determined me to pursue the resolution I had first taken. When he persisted and seized the bundle in my left hand, and endeavoring to take it by force, I wrenched it from him. But afterwards, when he used abusive language and threatened to kick me, I felt my indignation kindled to that degree, that I am glad I had so far command of myself as only to put myself in an attitude of defence, and say, you dare not. I have now lived fifty years, and this is the first time I ever received such an insult.[13]

The records of Congress fail to show that any notice was taken of the charges made by Laurens and Thomson against each other. The feud between the two patriots did not long continue, for on June 17, 1784, Thomson wrote to Laurens, congratulating him on the recovery of his

_____

12. Ibid., p. 264.
13. Ibid., p. 269.

health, and giving, at the same time, an interesting account of our foreign relations.

Thomson knew better than any other man the secret history of Congress and the motives which influenced its members. In his position, he beheld the national consciousness slowly develop, and he was present at the dawn of independence. Deborah Logan, a girl of fifteen at the time of the Declaration of Independence, has left an interesting description of how it was read to the people on July 8th. She had climbed up on the garden fence to get sight of what was going on, but the view was obstructed by a low frame building in Independence Square, which had been erected for astronomical purposes. Her recollections are as follows:

> How a little time spreads the mantle of oblivion over the most
> important events! It is now a matter of doubt at what hour
> or how the Declaration was given to the people; perhaps few
> remain who heard it read on that day; of those few, I am one,
> being in the lot adjoining to our old mansion in Chestnut Street,
> that then extended to Fifth. I distinctly heard the words of that
> instrument read to the people (I think from the State-house
> steps, for I did not see the speaker). . . . I think it was Charles
> Thomson's voice. It took place a little after twelve at noon, and
> they then proceeded down the street (I understood) to read it at
> the Courthouse. It was a time of fearful doubt, and great anxiety
> with the people, many of whom were appalled at the boldness of
> the measure, and the first audience of the Declaration was neither
> very numerous, nor composed of the most respectable class of
> citizens.[14]

After the Declaration of Independence, Congress began to deteriorate in quality, and it finally expired for want of a majority in October 1788. It was Thomson's opinion that no later Congress could compare with the first one in ability and patriotism. He regarded the Congress

---

14. Worthy Women of Our First Century, p. 283.

that met at York, Pennsylvania, while Washington's army was encamped at Valley Forge, a body of weak men with selfish motives.[15] As early as February 1778, the number of members was greatly reduced, and nearly all the men of superior abilities had disappeared. In January 1778, Laurens said: "A most shameful deficiency in this branch is the greatest evil, and is, indeed, the source of almost all our evils. If there is not speedily a resurrection of able men, and of that virtue which I thought to be genuine in seventy-five, we are gone. We shall undo ourselves."

Washington also deplored the fact that the States did not send able men to Congress, and in March 1779, he wrote: "Friends and foes seem now to combine to pull down the goodly fabric we have been raising at the expense of so much time, blood and treasure."

The deplorable condition of Congress was a fair indication of the state of affairs throughout the whole country. In April 1779, a paper dollar was worth five cents, and in many respects, this year marked the lowest ebb in politics and morals that was reached during the war. Robert Morris truly said:

> We are disputing about liberties, posts, and places at the very time we ought to have nothing in view but the securing of those objects and placing them on such a footing as to make them worth contending for among ourselves hereafter. But instead of this, the vigor of this and several other States is lost in intestine divisions; and unless the spirit of contention is checked by some other means, I fear it will have a baneful influence on the measures of America.

---

15. Rivington's Gazette, a Tory paper, December 21, 1777, gives the following account of the adjournment of Congress from Philadelphia to York: "As soon as the rebels learned that the British fleet was at the head of the Chesapeake, a motion was made in the Congress for an adjournment to some place 'at least one hundred miles from any part of God's Kingdom where the British mercenaries can possibly land,' which, after some rapturous demonstrations, was carried nem. con. Immediately the Congress commenced the retreat, leaving old nosey Thomson to pick up the duds and write promises to pay (when Congress should return) the Congress debts. In the flight, as in the rebellion, Hancock, having a just apprehension of the vengeance which awaits him, took the initiative and was the first to carry out the letter of the motion of his associates."

The depreciation of the currency was followed by an unusual rise in prices, commodities selling at Philadelphia in March 1780, at four times what they were in September preceding. In October 1780, Thomson wrote John Jay the following account of the extremities of the country:

> Upon this our enemies took courage and flattering themselves that Congress must sink under these embarrassments, they set every engine to work to continue and increase them, by counterfeiting the currency, multiplying their emissaries to decry its credit, tampering with our army and at the same time prosecuting the war with a greater degree of vigor than they had done from the commencement of it. To the honor of our country, I must inform you that history cannot produce such instances of fortitude, patience, and perseverance as were exhibited by our virtuous army. Though exposed to hunger and nakedness amidst the rigors of a most inclement winter, they struggled through with unparalleled firmness, and notwithstanding the tempting bribes and offers of the enemy, and the incredible hardships our soldiers suffered, the desertions were comparatively few.[16]

Thomson looked upon the financial distress of the colonies with the calmness of a philosopher. What a world of thought there is in the following words of the venerable Secretary:

> I would just observe, that if old established nations, populous, rich, and powerful, whose governments are fixed, whose revenues are settled, who have armies raised and fleets equipped, whose towns are fortified and whose arsenals and magazines are stored with implements and necessaries for war, if such nations find themselves under difficulties for want of money by one or two years' war with a nation weakened and greatly exhausted, what wonder if a young Commonwealth, whose inhabitants are poor

---

16. Collections of the New York Historical Society for the year 1878, p. 33.

and thinly scattered over a large extent of country, which was just emerging from the difficulties of settling a wilderness, and which being without arms, ammunition or military stores and without any established government what wonder if such a nation, under such circumstances forced into a way with one of the most powerful nations in the world should, after carrying on that war for six years with no other revenue than the voluntary contributions of the people, find itself embarrassed in its finances and under a necessity for applying for aid to other nations whose interest it is to humble the power with which it is contending.[17]

Through all these vicissitudes, Thomson's faith in the American cause remained unshaken. Franklin repeatedly tried to have his accounts with the government audited, but his efforts never met with any response from Congress. In 1788 he hinted to Thomson that republics are apt to be ungrateful, but Thomson never lost hope. On one occasion, he remarked to Franklin that it was no wonder that the States were backward, as everything was new and unusual. He expressed great confidence in the good sense of his countrymen and said: "Though you and I have lived to see a great work accomplished, yet much remains to be done to secure the happiness of this country."

As the revolution proceeded, Thomson was required to perform many of the duties that are now more appropriately the Secretary of State's business. He kept the "Secret Journal of Foreign Affairs," and had charge of the correspondence with our representatives abroad. John Jay wrote to him in 1781, while Minister to Madrid: "I wish in my heart that you were not only Secretary of Congress, but Secretary also for Foreign Affairs. I should then have better sources of information than gazettes and reports."

Thomson's letters to our foreign ministers contain much valuable information on the state of the country. On June 18, 1784, he wrote to John Jay:

---

17. Ibid., p. 33.

I have the pleasure to inform you that on the 7th of May Congress elected you Secretary of Foreign Affairs. I do not know how you will be pleased with the appointment but this I am aware of, that your country stands in need of your abilities in that office. I feel sensibly that it is not only time, but highly necessary for us to think and act like a sovereign as well as a free people, and I wish this sentiment were more deeply impressed on the members of every State in the Union. The opportunities you will have of corresponding not only with the executives, but with the several legislatures, in discharging the duties of your office, will I trust, greatly contribute to raise and promote this spirit. And this is a reason why I wish you were here to enter on the business. On the same day that you were elected to the office for foreign affairs, Congress appointed Mr. Jefferson in addition to Mr. J. Adams and Mr. B. Franklin for the purpose of negotiating commercial treaties with the powers of Europe.

Probably the most interesting of Thomson's letters is the one of August 13, 1784, to Dr. Franklin, who was then abroad. This letter, the original of which is among the Thomson papers in the library of Historical Society of Pennsylvania, gives a lengthy review of the political condition of the Union. On account of its important bearing upon Revolutionary history, it is given in full:

Dr. Franklin,
My Dear Friend:
    The renewal of our ancient correspondence and receipt of your letter excited those sensations which real friends feel on meeting unexpectedly after a long separation. As Mr. Jefferson, who I hope is by this time safe arrives, will explain matters to you and make you fully acquainted with the state of our affairs, I shall no longer conceal from you the circumstance of the omission of the signature of letter on June 7th last, which procured me the favor of hearing from you oftener than I had done. The letter was

to have been signed by the President as the latter was on the point of sailing, and the captain only waiting for the dispatch. I copied the letter in Congress and delivered it to the President, who sealed it up in a hurry without putting his name to it. So that my letters to you are all private, and this will explain the reason why they generally contain nothing of public affairs. I am sensible you must have been for a considerable time past greatly at a loss for want of official communications, and though I often wished to give you some, yet I forbore for reasons which if ever I shall be so happy as to have a personal interview I can express, which I am persuaded you will deem satisfactory. But this inconvenience will be obviated if Mr. Jay, who was with his family arrived at New York the 24th of July, and who as I mentioned to you in a former letter, is appointed Secretary of Foreign Affairs, accepts that office as I hope he will. Though I must confess my hope is founded more on my wishes than on any solid reason. I have written and informed him of his appointment and urged his acceptance but have not yet received his answer.

Colonel Harmer, who arrived with the Marquis de la Fayette after a fine passage of thirty-five days, delivered me on the 8th instant your letter of the 14th of June, with a copy of that of the 13th of May, which I had received before, announcing the exchange of the ratification of the definitive treaty of peace; on this happy completion of our hazardous enterprise I most sincerely congratulate you. It is an event which I have devoutly wished, and yet I cannot but say, the prospect of it has often excited many uneasy apprehensions. From the first appeal to arms, and through the whole contest, I never had a doubt of the issue, but I was afraid it would come upon us before we were prepared to receive it, and before we had acquired national principles, habits and sentiments which would enable us to improve it to advantage and to act becoming our station and dignity. I need not mention to you who know so well the peculiar circumstances of America at the commencement of this revolution. The several

colonies were distinct and separate governments, each jealous of
another, and kept apart by local interests and prejudices. Being
wholly dependent on Great Britain, they were secluded from
all intercourse with foreign nations. Having never been much
taxed, nor for any length of time they had no funds whereon to
ground public credit. Those who know the difficulty which old
established nations experience in their attempts to introduce new
arrangements either in government, police, or finance, will readily
conceive what we have had to encounter, more especially when
it is considered that the ancient governments being dissolved,
the people were thrown into a state of nature, that property
being equally divided, and the feudal system unknown in this
country, there were no individuals to whom the people were
accustomed to look up and who could influence their conduct
or opinions. And even when new governments were adopted,
the ideas of liberty which prevailed, threw the whole power into
the hands of the people, and the rotation which took place in
the legislatures and executives of the several states afforded little
opportunity of acquiring national sentiments. Notwithstanding
all this, we have made considerable progress in the short space of
eight years, the time elapsed since we became a nation, and I am
happy to think that the people every day become more and more
impressed with the necessity of honorably discharging our debts,
supporting public credit, and establishing a national character.
And though Rhode Island still holds out and refuses her assent to
the impost of five percent, yet as all the other states have agreed
to the measure. I have strong hopes that she may be induced to
come into it, or that some means will be devised to overcome the
obstacle which her refusal throws in the way. In like manner, I am
persuaded the people of these states will quickly find it to be their
interest as well as of absolute necessity to be faithful in the obser-
vance of treaties and to avoid internal contentions and divisions.

There is no doubt but Great Britain will watch for advantages,
if not to recover what she has lost, at least to be revenged for

what she has suffered. And that everything will be attempted, and every sacrifice used which malice can suggest to break our connection with France and sow dissensions among the stats. The easy access which foreigners have to these states and the ready reception they meet with afford favorable opportunities of putting their arts in practice. And it is worthy of observation that it is strangers lately come among us whom we know nothing of, joined with men who, to say the least of them, were lukewarm in our cause and of doubtful characters, who are now most active in sowing jealousies of France from an affected regard for our liberty, and a zeal to preserve this country from foreign influence. I think it therefore highly necessary both for France and America to be on their guard and not to suffer themselves to be duped by the arts of their common enemy.

The atrocious unprovoked outrage lately committed in this city by one Longchamps, a vagabond Frenchman, seems to carry strong marks of a premeditated design to embroil us with France, and what makes this still more probably, is the palliating account given of this affair in a paper newly set up here as if for the purpose, entitled the *Courier de l'Amerique*, which is conducted by Bonoid and Gaillard, who came to this place last fall about the same time as Longchamps. The whole complexion of this paper evidences a marked inveteracy against France and a strong desire to excite fears and jealousies, or at least to give an unfavorable impression of her. I am glad to find that the zeal of the authors has hurried them into a palpable manifestation of their design, and that suspicions are already raised which I trust will guard against the influence of the poison they mean to convey.

I send you the *Courier de l'Amerique* as far as published, and some other papers of the day, which will explain the circumstances of the outrage committed by Longchamps and the measures taken by the government, and in consequence thereof, I must inform you that the judges have not yet given an answer to the last letter of the President. The question whether

Longchamps can be legally delivered up by Council according to the claim made by the late Minister of France, was publicly argued by lawyers before the Judges, who still have it under advisement. In the meanwhile, Longchamps is confined in prison. The matter is laid before the legislature who have now under consideration a bill which I have no doubt they will pass, effectually securing the rights and immunities of public ministers and punishing the violators of them.

It may not be amiss to acquaint you that from his own showing, it appears that Longchamps had been an officer in the French service; that in 1776, he came to America and went to our camp before Boston, where he was cordially received; that after being in our camp and about headquarters for some weeks, he took advantage of a pass given for the purpose of going to the country, to slip into Boston, which we were besieging; that he wanted permission of General Gage to come again into our camp, but for some reason that does not appear, it was not granted. In short, from any circumstances there is reason to suspect that at a time he either was or wished to be employed as a spy by the British General. Whether his late crime is the effect of sudden passion or the result of premeditated plan may possibly in time be manifested.

There is a circumstance in the conduct of Longchamps not mentioned in any of the papers, which it may not be improper to inform you of. On the 17th, he committed the first insult; on the 18th, he went to a justice of the peace and took an oath of allegiance to the State, after which he perpetrated the outrage of the 19th. His views in taking the oath have been variously interpreted, some imagining that he meant hereby to secure himself from the French laws and from the power and resentment of the consul; others that his design was by becoming a citizen to involve the State in his crime, and interest the populace in his favor. But whatever might have been his views even the lawyers who undertook his defense laid little stress upon it in their pleadings, and the bench seemed to be decidedly of the opinion that the oath he had taken was of no effect, and that he was to be considered only in the light of an alien stranger.

The combination which Mr. Jefferson carried with him, and which I hope you have received before this, will not only inform you of the purpose of Congress respecting your request of recall but enable you to satisfy the Danish minister and to proceed on commercial treaties with Great Britain and other powers. I wish I were able to give you pleasing expectations with respect to some employment for your Secretary W.T.F., against whose conduct or abilities while in public service, I have never heard the least objection; on the contrary, I have always heard them well spoken of. But to me it appears that it will be injuring your grandson to delay making some other provision for him in hope of an employment from Congress, and of this I am persuaded you are already convinced by the appointment of Col. Humphreys; and yet I have seen such changes in the conduct of public affairs, occasioned by the change of men entrusted with the direction of them, that there is always room left for hope. But he who has other means of support is less affected by a disappointment in meeting with public employ, and if his country stands in need of his services and calls upon him to fill any office, he seems to confer rather than to receive an obligation by accepting it.

I have taken some steps, but they have hitherto been fruitless, to find out Philip Hearn. Upon inquiry, I learn that Holland came to this country in 1775, and he was employed as Adjutant to a regiment; that in 1776 he was promoted to the rank of Captain in the Delaware regiment and was killed in the battle of Germantown in 1777; that he married a daughter of Parson Ross, of Delaware State, by whom he left issue, and that his widow and children enjoy a pension from the Assembly of the State agreeably to a recommendation of Congress. I need not mention with what marks of cordiality and affection the Marquis de la Fayette,

who came to this place last Monday, was received by all ranks
of people. His stay was short, as he was anxious to see General
Washington. He left town this morning and expects to be back in
three or four weeks. Mr. Laurens is arrived at New York, but not
yet come forward. I intended to have troubled Mr. Jefferson with
a line by this opportunity, but my letter to you has insensibly
become so long that I shall not have time. You will please to
make my respectful compliments to him and to Mr. Adams.

    With sincere affection and esteem,

    I am, Dear Sir,

    Your old friend,

    Charles Thomson

On April 26, 1784, Congress decided to adjourn from June 3d, to
meet at Trenton on October 30th, following. The permanent session of
Congress and the members' carelessness had created much uneasiness
throughout the country, while some of the States recommended peri-
odical sessions. Jefferson and other leading statesmen favored a recess in
the interests of economy, as well as to invigorate the government. The
Confederation had not been organized into separate departments, but
it was provided in the Articles of Confederation that the management
of public affairs should be in charge of the Committee of the States
when Congress was not in session. This executive board consisted of
one member from each State, and its powers were to embrace all the
executive functions of Congress. The concurrence of nine members was
required on all questions, except that of adjournment from day to day. A
Journal was to be kept, published monthly, and forwarded to the several
States, among other regulations. The Committee met at Annapolis on
June 4th and elected Mr. S. Hardy chairman. As it was necessary for
Thomson to return to Philadelphia, he was granted a leave of absence,
while Messrs. Bankson and Remsen were appointed to act as clerks in his
place. The Committee then adjourned to meet again on June 26th, but it

was impossible to get representatives present from nine States until June 8th.[18] Efforts were then made to have the Committee assemble either at Trenton or Philadelphia. On August 3d, three of the members returned home, and it appears that nothing was accomplished even as late as October 1st, for Thomson wrote on that date: "But it does appear to me that any Committee will be formed before the meeting of Congress, which is to be at Trenton on the 30th of this month."

During his absence, Thomson kept in close touch with the Committee of Annapolis. On June 20th, 1784, he wrote to Mr. Hardy, the chairman:

> Pursuant to the order of Congress, I prepared three commissioners for our ministers for negotiating treaties with the commercial powers of Europe, one empowering them to negotiate additional treaties of commerce with France, conformable to the instructions given, another doing the same with the United Netherlands, and a third for the like purpose of Sweden. These, I forwarded yesterday together with the duplicate of the instructions given May 30th and October 29th, 1783, the answer of Congress of October 29th, to the letter from the Burgomasters and Senate of the imperial free city of Hamburg, the act of November 1st, 1783, the act of March 16th, 1784, on the letters of November 1st and December 25th from Doctor Franklin, the instructions of the 7th and 11th of last month and those given on the 3d instant, which comprehend the whole business now before them; and for their further information, I have forwarded to them a copy of the Journal of the last session of Congress up to May 28th, and a newspaper containing the ordinance for putting the treasury into

---

18. "The scheme was found to be an impracticable one, though it was the best within the authority of Congress at that time to adopt. And on the whole, it was a happy circumstance for our Republic, that the theory proved as impracticable as it did; for it developed, in a clear light, the palpable defect of the confederation, in not having provided for a separation of the legislative, executive and judiciary functions; and this defect, together with the want of adequate powers in the general government to collect their contributions and to regulate commerce, was the great cause which led to the formation and adoption of our present constitution." – Life of Thomas Jefferson, by B. L. Rayner, p. 206.

commission, and the appointment and powers of the Committee of the States.

Thomson was greatly disappointed that the Committee should remain at Annapolis, while there were several more suitable places where its sessions might be held. He wrote to Mr. Read, of South Carolina, July 23, 1784, expressing his displeasure, as follows:

> I acknowledge, my dear sir, the beauties and agreeable situation
> of Annapolis, and will admit that the graces and charms of its
> nymphs are not excelled by those of the inhabitants of Calypso's
> isle. And were you and your associates in pursuit only of love
> and pleasure, I would allow there is no place where you could
> more properly fix your habitation. But these are not the objects
> of the patriot's pursuit. The dance, the ball, and continued round
> of pleasure are not the means of promoting the interests of his
> country, regarding its rights, and advancing its happiness and
> prosperity. I confess, therefore, I should not be sorry if some kind
> of monster, I care not whether in the form of a mosquito, or a
> fever and ague were to drive you from that enchanting place into
> the walks of politics, and force you to turn your attention to the
> concerns of this young and rising empire which demands your
> care.

When Mr. Bankson wrote to Thomson on August 13, 1784, that the dissolution of the Committee was imminent, the old patriot was filled with indignation, and he at once addressed the following note to Mr. Hardy:

> Can it be possible that gentlemen will take such a rash step as
> to dissolve the Committee and leave the United States without
> any head or visible authority? Have they considered what may
> be the consequences? At this moment, if I am rightly informed,

there is a war carrying on between the people of Connecticut
and Pennsylvania and Wyoming. The frontiers are in a state
of anxiety respecting the disposition of the Indians. Who is to
convene the States if the Committee is dissolved? If Annapolis
is become inconvenient or dangerous on account of the sickly
season approaching, could not the Committee have adjourned to
this place or Trenton?

During the last five years of his public life, the letters of Thomson
have but little bearing upon the politics of the day. He frequently wrote
to Jefferson and other prominent statesmen, but chiefly upon scientific
subjects, which I shall treat in a subsequent chapter. In closing this review of Thomson's political career, I cannot refrain from calling attention
to his shrewdness and wisdom as a leader. He had no time to harangue
the people on the eternal rights of a man, a pursuit that would only
tend to increase factional strife. His opportunity lay in the committee
of correspondence and in the secret deliberations of Congress; for as
Sydney George Fisher remarked, "This child of liberty which they were
nursing could bear no noise."[19] Thomson described his political methods
in a letter to Hon. J. Montgomery, August 22, 1784. He said: "I have
received your favor of the 2d in which you seem to think hard of your
not receiving an answer to your letter on C.'s affair. I thought by this time
your experience had taught you that there are mysteries in government
which little folks are not to be permitted to pry into, and which are only
to be communicated to such as are deeply skilled in what the *wise* King
James used to call *kingcraft*."

Thomson maintained a secret correspondence with a few trusted
friends, who transmitted to him on several occasions valuable information concerning the enemy. Mrs. Write, the celebrated modeler in wax,
was particularly active in this direction, and it was through intelligence

---

19. Pennsylvania: Colony and Commonwealth, p. 299.

given by her that the military store ships were captured.[20] Thomson had an understanding with Rivington,[21] the King's printer at New York, who informed him of a plot to poison General Washington while quartered on the Hudson River. Some authorities state that Thomson was poisoned while there and owed his recovery to the excellence of his constitution.

The time had now arrived for Thomson to sever his relations with Congress. The Constitution's adoption brought other men into prominence, while many of the leading figures of the Revolutionary period retired from the cares of public life. Thomson was always treated most graciously by Congress. As no compensation was received for the first service, that body presented him with a silver urn, inscribed as their gift, and also as a compliment to his wife. Mrs. Thomson was consulted to learn what the present should be, and she chose an urn.

Postscript – Since the completion of this chapter, the following letter, written by Thomson, was found in the collections of the Historical Society of Pennsylvania. It is published here with the permission of the Society.

Annapolis, Jan. 7, 1784.
To Richard Peters, Esq.:
Considering what a deep share I have taken in this controversy and how anxious I have ever been not only for the success of our

---

20. Mrs. Write was an ardent republican, and a story is told of her that while in London, the King inquired of her how it would be possible to restore the colonies to allegiance. She replied: "Friends you may make them, but never subjects. For America, before a King can reign there, must become a wilderness, without other inhabitants than the beasts of the forest. The opponents of the decrees of your Parliament, rather than submit, would perish to a man; but if the restoration of peace be seriously the object of your wishes, I am confident that it needs but the striking off of three heads to produce it."

"And whose are the three heads to be struck off, madam?"

"Oh, Lord North's and Lord George Germaine's, beyond all question."

"And who's the third head?"

"Oh, Sire, politeness forbids me to name him. Your Majesty could never wish me to forget myself and be guilty of an incivility."

21. It was a matter of universal surprise, on the return of peace, that this most obnoxious man remained after the departure of the British troops. But the surprise soon ceased, by its becoming publicly known that he had been a spy for General Washington, while employed in abusing him, and had impaired useful information, which could not otherwise have been obtained." – Life of Rev. Ashbel Green, by Rev. J. H. Jones, p. 45.

cause, but for the honor and dignity of the United States, you will readily conceive that a recollection of the events which have taken place these six months past must give me the most pungent pain. During the contest, I have been witness to scenes which gave me extreme uneasiness and distress, but I had this consolation that we had an object which engaged the attention of foreign nations, an army and a general struggling with difficulties, and in spite of cold and hunger, bearing up against and checking a powerful invading foe, and sometimes gaining important advantages. But now that the war is closed with honor and success, the eyes of all Europe are turned upon that council, which, it was supposed, directed the measures of their continent, in high expectation of seeing traits of wisdom, dignity and prudence, and what a scene have they exhibited! Oh, that it could be obliterated from the annals of America and utterly effaced from my memory! You will judge of the feeling of some of the members by an expression which Mr. Read used in a late speech. 'While Congress,' said he, 'are vagabondizing from one paltry village to another, it is impossible for gentlemen to have recourse to books or to consult writers on the laws of nations.'

The opening of the First Continental Congress

Peyton Randolph

John Adams

Roger Sherman

Patrick Henry

Robert Morris

John Jay

Henry Laurens

chapter 6

Close of His Political Career

*T*homson's political career drew to a close with the death of the old Continental Congress, and his mission to Mount Vernon in April 1789. A quorum being present in the United States Senate for the first time on April 6th, that body "appointed Charles Thomson, Esq., to notify George Washington, Esq., of his election to the office of President of the United States."[1]

Thomson set out for Mount Vernon on April 7th, and having reached his destination on the 14th,[2] he communicated the purport of his mission to Washington in the following words:

> Sir, the President of the Senate, chosen for the special purpose, having opened and counted the votes of the electors in the presence of the Senate and House of Representatives, I was honored with the commands of the Senate to wait upon your Excellency with the information of your being elected to the office of

---

1. The Debates and Proceedings in the Congress of the United States, Vol. 1, p. 17.

2. "In April 1789, the doors of Mount Vernon opened to receive, and Washington hastened to embrace, the venerable Charles Thomson, the Secretary to the Continental Congress during fifteen consecutive years. He came charged with the important duty of announcing to the retired General his unanimous election to the office of President of the United States. The tall, attenuated form, the simple yet dignified manners of Secretary Thomson made him a most favored guest at a board where had been welcomed many of the wise, the good, the brave, and renowned." – Recollections and Private Memoirs of Washington, by his adopted son, George Washington Parke Custis.

THE LIFE OF CHARLES THOMSON

President of the United States of America. This commission was intrusted to me on account of my having been long in the confidence of the late Congress and charged with the duties of one of the principal civil departments of the Government. I have now, sir, to inform you that the proofs you have given of your patriotism and your readiness to sacrifice domestic ease and private enjoyments to preserve the happiness of your country did not permit the two Houses to harbor a doubt of your undertaking this great and important office, to which you are called, not only by the unanimous vote of the electors, but by the voice of America.

I have it, therefore, in command to accompany you to New York, where the Senate and House of Representatives are convened for the dispatch of public business.

To which Washington replied as follows: "I wish that there may not be reason for regretting the choice for, indeed, all I can promise is to accomplish that which can be done by honest zeal."

Immediate preparations were made for the eventful journey to New York, for on April 16th, Washington made the following entry in his diary:

About ten o'clock I bade adieu to Mount Vernon, to private life, and to domestic felicity, and with a mind oppressed with more anxious and painful sensations than I have words to express, set out for New York in company with Mr. Thomson and Colonel Humphreys, with the best disposition to render service to my country in obedience to its calls, but with less hope of answering its expectations.[3]

After an eventful journey, the party reached New York City on April 23rd, and the next day Thomson sent a letter to the Hon. John Langdon, President of the Senate, informing him that he had delivered General

3. Washington After the Revolution, by William S. Baker, p. 121.

Washington the certificate of his being elected President of the United States.[4] During the week following, congress was busy in preparing for the inaugural ceremonies to be held on April 30th. It appears that Thomson's name was omitted from the program of the day, for William Maclay wrote on April 29, 1789: "Charles Thomson has, however, been ill-used by the Committee of Arrangements on the ceremonial. This is wrong. His name has been left out of the arrangements for to-morrow."[5]

The next day, April 30th, Mr. Reed arose in the Senate and called the attention of the members to the neglect that had been shown Thomson. Mr. Lee attempted to answer him, but the confusion being so great, Maclay could not hear a word he said.[6]

Thomson was somewhat disappointed at his treatment by the new government. It is evident that he expected an appointment, for on April 7, 1789, he wrote to Robert Morris:

> I am afraid they rate my abilities too high. Sure, I am they rate them much higher than I do myself, and more than they deserve. But such as they are, to show that I am not unwilling to devote them to the public service, I will make this proposition: That the keeping of the Great Seal, with the duties thereto annexed, and to be annexed, and the custody and care of the papers, which belonged to the late Congress, be committed to me, this office to be made the depository of the acts, laws, and archives of Congress; that the same salary be continued to me which the late Congress granted me, and my style be Secretary of the Senate of the United States or Congress; and besides necessary clerks, I be allowed a Deputy, who if it be the pleasure of the Senate, may be nominated or appointed by themselves, to do the ordinary business of the House, so that I may not be under the necessity of attending except on social occasions and when the great business of the

---

4. The original of Thomson's letter to Mr. Langdon, describing his visit to Mount Vernon, as well as General Washington's reply, was afterwards presented to the American Philosophical Society. This letter was purloined from the Society's library by some unknown person.

5. Journal of William Maclay, United States Senator from Pennsylvania, 1789-1791.

6. Sketches of Debate in the First Senate of the United States, by William Maclay, p. 15.

nation is under deliberation. If this proposition be approved by
the Senate and acceptable, I am ready to serve them to the utmost
of my power, at least till the present government be organized.[7]

There is no record that Thomson's proposition was ever considered
into the Senate. His friends could have influenced the Senate to appoint
him Secretary of that body, but he desired the additional powers and
titles as outlined in his letter to Morris. Maclay's Journal, July 13, 1789,
gives the following account of Thomson's political ambitions at that time:

> I forgot to minute yesterday that, late in the afternoon, Charles
> Thomson visited me. We had much chat of the political kind. He
> showed a great disposition to go into the field of the President's
> power. He was clearly of the opinion that the President ought to
> remove all officer's etc. Indeed, he said so much on the subject
> that I had like to have entertained a suspicion that he came on
> purpose to sound, or rather, prepare me on the subject. I agreed
> to sundry of his observations, at the same time dissented in plain
> but not pointed terms from some other things. Perhaps this is the
> best way, on the whole, for an independent man to act. Honestly,
> on the whole, is the best policy. I really feel for Mr. Thomson's
> situation. A man who has been the graphic faculty of the old
> Congress, and who – I feel a kind of certainty of the fact – wishes
> to die in an eminent office, would not suffer his friends to
> continue him Secretary of the Senate, and his enemies have taken
> advantage of it, and declared him out of office, and mean to keep
> him so. It was certainly bad policy for him to refuse the offer of
> his friends. The political door is harder to be opened than any
> other if once it is thrown in a man's face.

On July 24, 1789, Thomson wrote to Washington, expressing his
determination to return to private life; but at the same time, he confessed

---

7. Collections of the New York Historical Society for the Year 1878, p. 249.

that he should have been highly gratified to devote himself to the public service under the new administration. Washington at once replied, describing his feelings of regret in the following beautiful language:

> The present age does so much justice to the unsullied reputation with which you have always conducted yourself in the execution of the duties of your office, and posterity will find your name so honorably connected with the unification of such a multitude of astonishing facts that my single suffrage would add little to the illustration of your merits. Yet I cannot without any just testimonial in favor of so old, so faithful, and so able a public officer, which might tend to sooth his mind in the shades of retirement. Accept, then, this serious declaration that your services have been important as your patriotism was distinguished; and enjoy that best of all rewards, the consciousness of having done your duty well.[8]

In reply to this tribute, Thomson said:

> Sir, I cannot find words to express the feelings of my heart on receipt of your favor of yesterday; from the love and veneration I have, and have continually felt for you, and the light in which I have always viewed you as raised up by Providence to be the savior and father of our country, I freely confess I should have been highly gratified in devoting myself to the public service under your administration. But by attentively observing and weighing circumstances and occurrences, it appeared to me to be the will of God that I should return to private life. Under this impression, though, I wish not merely to submit, but to submit with cheerfulness, I own I felt an uneasiness at the circumstances you mention, and which you are pleased to say you have to regret that the period of your coming again into public life should be exactly that in which I am to retire from it. But, sir, you know it

---

8. Ibid., p. 250.

is not from any unwillingness to serve under you. I thank you for
the testimonial you have given in my favor, and shall ever prize it
next to the consciousness of having done my duty to my country
to the utmost of my knowledge and abilities.

By direction of Washington, Thomson delivered the books, records,
and papers of the Continental Congress, the Great Seal of the Federal
Union, and the Seal of the Admiralty of Mr. Roger Alden, late Deputy
Secretary of Congress, who was requested to take care of them. Almost
fifteen years had been passed in the service of his country, through a most
eventful period, and his retirement could not fail to attract considerable
attention. In the *Gazette of the United States*, July 25, 1789, appeared the
following notice:

> On Thursday last, that venerable patriot Charles Thomson, Esq.,
> resigned to the President of the United States his office of Sec-
> retary of Congress – a post which he has filled for nearly fifteen
> years, with reputation to himself and advantage to his country.
>
> When Heav'n propitious smiled upon our arms,
> Or scenes adverse spread terror and alarms,
> Through every change the Patriot was the same –
> And Faith and Hope attended Thomson's name.

Some of his most intimate friends freely discussed Thomson's disappointment on his failure to secure a high office in the new government.
Timothy Pickering visited him in December 1789 and made the following observations: "On the arrangement of the new government, no office
was provided for him. He retired from Congress about August last, I
think somewhat chagrined. But this will wear off; and, as he and his wife
have a competent fortune, they will live more happily than ever in their
present retirement."[9]

---

9. The Life of Timothy Pickering, by Charles W. Upham, Vol. 2, p. 436.

There is no evidence that Thomson made any further efforts to secure political honors, except a rumor of which Maclay wrote in his Journal on December 6, 1790. He said: "My brother informed me this morning that Charles Thomson had applied to one Collins, a member from Berks County, for his interest to obtain my place as Senator. It comes very direct, and was talked over yesterday at Blair McClenachan's, where Matthew Irwin dined, from whom my brother (Samuel Maclay) had it."

If Thomson had aspirations for the senatorship, the fact did not become generally known. On February 28, 1793, the Pennsylvania Legislature elected Albert Gallatin as Maclay's successor in the Senate, and during the whole canvass, Thomson's name was not suggested.

In January 1793, the Western Indians proposed a conference with the government, at Sandusky, for the purpose of treating on peace. Thomson's wide experience in Indian affairs naturally induced Washington to nominate him as one of the commissioners. In urging him to accept this responsible duty, Washington said:

> It is necessary that characters be appointed who are known to
> our citizens for their talent and integrity, and whose situation
> in life places them clear of suspicion of a wish to prolong the
> war, and whose interest in common with that of their country is
> clearly to produce peace. Characters inviting these desiderata do
> not abound, and in fact, many circumstances circumscribe their
> choice within a small circle.

As Thomson declined this honor, the President finally nominated Benjamin Lincoln, Beverly Randolph, and Timothy Pickering to serve as commissioners. The venerable Secretary of Congress now felt that the hand of kind Providence was guiding him into other pursuits, and he followed with all the resignation of a true patriot.

Early painting of Mount Vernon

Charles Thomson delivers the election results to George Washington at Mount Vernon.

George Washington

US Great Seal, Charles Thomson preliminary design

chapter seven

Interest in Science—Relations with His "Ancient Friend," Jefferson— Observations on the Notes of the State of Virginia

hroughout his life, Thomson had an absorbing interest in science. He was elected to membership in the American Philosophical Society on September 22, 1758; was Secretary of the society from 1769 to 1770 and served as one of its councilors from 1781 to 1783. He was active in the deliberations of that body and was frequently appointed on some of its most important committees. On May 20, 1769, he was selected, with Messrs. Ewing and Williamson, to wait on Miss Norris, and request the use of the telescope in her possession, on the occasion of the transit of Venus, June 3d, of that year. The society erected an observatory in the State House yard to view the transit, and Thomson was deeply interested in this event, as is shown by the following account in the *Pennsylvania Gazette*, June 8, 1769:

> We hear that the Committee appointed by the American
> Philosophical Society for the Promotion of Useful Knowledge, to
> observe the transit of Venus, which happened on Saturday last,
> having distributed themselves into three classes, Rev. Mr. John

Ewing, Joseph Shippen, Esq., Dr. Hugh Williamson, Messrs. Thomas Prior, Charles Thomson, and James Pearson, observed at the public observatory in the State House Square; the Rev. Doctor William Smith, John Lukens, Esq., Messrs. David Rittenhouse and John Sellers, at Mr. Rittenhouse's observatory, at Norriton; and Mr. Owen Biddle, at the Light House near the Capes of Delaware. The weather was extremely favorable, and the observations at the three several places were completed greatly to the satisfaction of the observers. As soon as the Committees have digested their remarks to lay before the Society, we are promised an authentic account of the result of their observations, which we understand agree to great exactness with each other, making allowance for the difference of place, etc.

The society invited Thomson to deliver the anniversary oration in January 1774. Dr. Smith and Dr. Rush were appointed to inform him of the duty, but the honor was declined. On motion of Mr. Jefferson, at a meeting of the Society, April 15, 1791, Thomson was elected, with Messrs. Barton, Hutchinson, Wistar and Jefferson, to collect material for forming the natural history of the Hessian fly, and the best means for its prevention or destruction, and whatever else relative to the same of interest or agriculture.

Thomson's activities in the American Philosophical Society marked the beginning of a correspondence with Jefferson on scientific subjects, extending over many years.[1] Jefferson had a great passion for philosophy and the natural sciences, and he once declared that he preferred "the woods, the wilds, and the independence of Monticello to all the brilliant pleasures of the most brilliant courts in Europe."[2]

---

1. Jefferson was President of the Society for a number of years. "Of this Society he was the pride and ornament. He presided over it for a number of years with great efficiency, elevating its character, and extending its operations by those means which his enlarged acquaintance with science and the literary world enabled him to command. His constant attendance at its meetings, while he resided in Philadelphia, gave them an interest which had not been excited for a number of years. Science, under his auspices, received a fresh impulse, as will appear by consulting the Transactions of that period, which were enriched by many valuable contributions from himself." – Life of Thomas Jefferson, by. B. L. Rayner, p. 292.

2. Life of Thomas Jefferson, by B. L. Rayner, p. 191.

His life at Monticello in 1781 is pictured as follows by the French traveler, General Chastellux:

> Let me describe to you a man, not yet forty; tall, and with a mild and pleasing countenance, but whose mind and understanding are ample substitutions for every external grace – an American, who, without ever having quitted his own country, is at once a musician, skilled in drawing, a geometrician, an astronomer, a natural philosopher, legislator, and statesman – a Senator of America, who sat for two years in that famous Congress which brought about the revolution; and which is never mentioned without respect, though unhappily not without regret, – a Governor of Virginia, who filled this difficult station during the invasions of Arnold, of Phillips, and of Cornwallis – a philosopher in voluntary retirement from the world and public business, because he loves the world inasmuch only, as he can flatter himself with being useful to mankind; and the minds of his countrymen are not yet in a condition either to bear the light, or to suffer contradiction – a mild and amiable wife, charming children, of whose education he himself takes a charge, a house to embellish, great provisions, and the arts and sciences to cultivate; – these are what remain to Mr. Jefferson, after having played a principal character on the theatre of the new word, and which he preferred to the honorable commission of minister plenipotentiary in Europe.

Thomson had many traits of character in common with Jefferson. Both had served their country with distinction in the Revolutionary period and sacrificed the enjoyment of ease for the cares of public life. Both were men of sense and learning, representing the best scholarship of the day, and their interest was great in the advancement of the useful sciences. Both made substantial contributions to the sum of knowledge, Jefferson in the philosophy of government, and Thomson in Biblical literature. The correspondence between the two men from 1784 to 1787 is attended with a peculiar interest. Jefferson was in France during this period, and he kept his ancient friend constantly informed of the progress of science in the Old World. To Lafayette, he wrote in 1787:

> I am constantly roving about to see what I have never seen before
> and shall never see again. In the great cities, I go to see what
> travelers think alone worthy of being seen; but I make a job of it,
> and generally gulp it all down in a day. On the other hand, I am
> never satiated with rambling through the fields and farms, exam-
> ining the culture and cultivators with a degree of curiosity, which
> makes some take me to be a fool, and others to be much wiser
> than I am. . . . From the first olive fields of Pierrelotte, to the
> orangeries of Hieres, it has been continued rapture to me. I have
> often wished for you. I think you have not made this journey. It
> is a pleasure you have to come, and an improving to be added
> to the many you have already made. It will be a great comfort to
> you, to know, from your own inspection, the condition of all the
> provinces of your own country, and it will be interesting to them
> at some future day, to be known to you. This is, perhaps, the only
> moment of your life in which you can acquire that knowledge.
> And to do it most effectually, you must be absolutely *incognito*,
> you must ferret the people out of their hovels, as I have done,
> look into their kettles, eat their bread, loll on their beds under
> pretence of resting yourself, but in fact to find if they are soft.
> You will feel a sublime pleasure in the course of this investigation,
> and a sublime one hereafter, when you shall be able to apply
> your knowledge to the softening of their beds, or the throwing a
> morsel of meat into their kettle of vegetables.

Jefferson was continually meeting with fresh experiences and learning of new inventions and discoveries during his stay abroad. He was always prompt in communicating knowledge of them to Thomson. On November 11, 1784, he wrote:

I send you a pamphlet on the subject of animal magnetism, which has disturbed the nerves of prodigious numbers here. I believe this report will allay the evil. I also send you Roberts' last aerial voyage. There has been a lamp called the cylinder lamp lately invented here. It gives a light equal, as is thought, to that of six or eight candles. It requires olive oil, but its consumption is not great. The improvement is produced by forcing the wick into a hollow cylinder so that there is a passage for the air through the hollow. The idea had occurred to Doctor Franklin a year or two before, but he tried his experiment with a rush, which not succeeding he did not prosecute it. The fact was the rush formed too small a cylinder; the one used is of an inch diameter. They make shade candlesticks for studious men, which are excellent for reading; these cost two guineas. I should have sent you a specimen of the phosphoric matches but that I am told Mr. Rittenhouse has had some of them. They are a beautiful discovery and very useful, especially to heads which like yours and mine cannot at all times be got to sleep. The convenience of lighting a candle without getting out of bed, of sealing letters without calling a servant, of kindling a fire without flint, steel, punk, etc., are of value.[3]

While Jefferson resided in Paris, experiments were being made in the use of balloons, a full account of which he wrote to Thomson.[4] He also observed in London the application of steam as an agent for working grist mills. In a letter to Thomson, April 22, 1786, he said:

I have visited the one lately made here. It was at that time turning eight pair of stones. I do not know whether the quantity of fuel is to be increased. I hear you are applying this same agent in America to navigate boats, and I have little doubt but that it will

---

3. Collections of the New York Historical Society for the year 1878, p. 197.

4. "The balloon discovery has had a rapid rise and has been pursued with great spirit as a rare show. But unless some skillful artist can find out some way to direct its course and preserve the gas, I fear the remembrance of it will only furnish a figure in poetry and oratory, like Phaeton's attempt to guide the Chariot of the Sun." – Thomson to Jefferson, April 6, 1786.

be applied generally to machines so as to supersede the use of water ponds and of course to lay open all the streams for navigation. We know that steam is one of the most powerful engines we can employ, and in America fuel is abundant. I find no new publication here worth sending to you.

In replying to Jefferson's communications, Thomson remarked that his time was so engrossed with his office's duties that he had but little time for philosophical research. Often at night, however, if he chanced to awake, he would revolve in his mind "some subject which I wish to trace through its various relations or its probably effects and consequences."[5]

In 1785, he made an investigation into the nature of Mesmer's animal magnetism. Lafayette was enthusiastic on the subject, and being present at a meeting of the American Philosophical Society, he entertained the members with experiments the great part of the evening. Lafayette informed his audience that he was one of Mesmer's scholars, or initiates, and was let into the secret but was not at liberty to reveal it. Writing to Jefferson, March 6, 1785, Thomson made the following comments on these experiments: "Still, however, it appeared to me strange that there should be a fluid pervading all nature capable of being collected, and where he collected of producing such wondrous effects, and that no trace of it should ever before have been observed or noticed by any philosopher in the various researches into nature or the experiments on matter and motion."

In the summer of 1786, a remarkable display of the Northern Lights was visible in the eastern part of the United States. On July 6th of this year, Thomson wrote to Jefferson what is probably the best account of this phenomenon extant. In the course of his letter, he said:

During the course of last week, we have had here for several evenings a display of the northern lights. The wind had blown for some days from south-west, and the weather was warm and dry.

---

5. Collections of the New York Historical Society for the year 1878, p. 199.

As my house nearly fronts the S.S.W and has a large open back, I had a full and beautiful view of the lights from the windows of my back parlor, which is raised one story from the ground, the opposite houses only intercepting about four or five degrees from the horizon. As I viewed them on Friday, June 30th, there appeared over the tops of the houses a white luminous cloud extending in a horizontal position from N.E. to N.W. From this cloud at difference places darted up and successive streams of light tapering to points, some of them to the height of 50 degrees. The stars were bright and the north pole clearly discernible among the streamers, so that by it I could judge of their height. Sometimes the white cloud appeared, in which case I observed the ascending stream was tinged with red and continued to have a reddish hue. Having a lofty steeple in view to guide my eye and direct my judgment, I observed two or three of the streams which rose in the north-east and were of this hue, moving with a slow but regular progressive motion toward the north, still continuing perpendicular and very high.

From one of them I thought I saw a flash of lightning, but not seeing it repeated, I concluded I was mistaken. The light was so great as to cast a shadow from my body and from my hands against a wall. On the following evening, Saturday, July 1st, we had nearly the same appearance but not in so great a degree. These, you will observe, are only common phenomena which philosophers have endeavored to account for on various principles, and about which I should not have troubled you, but for the phenomenon which appeared on Saturday night. This was a luminous belt or stream of light, forming a great and regular bow from east to west. At what time it made its first appearance or how it was formed, whether instantaneously or by degrees, I cannot say, as I did not see its first formation. My attention was called to it about half after 10 o'clock. It was then quite complete and seemed to form an arch passing through the zenith from horizon to horizon. As I viewed it to the west it seemed to rise from behind the opposite houses like a stream of pale white light about a yard broad, spreading as it advanced to the zenith to two or three times that breadth. Viewed to the east it had the same appearance down to the horizon, where its breadth appeared the same as just over the tops of the houses to the west. I watched it for half an hour, during which time it continued invariably the same. At length to the east I saw it drawing to a point at the horizon and gradually abating in light for four or five degrees upwards. After it seemed to have vanished to that height or rather more, it darted down at short intervals from the luminous part, a pointed, quivering stream. Soon after the light began to abate through the whole circle. I did not continue to watch it till it wholly disappeared, as I was indisposed and afraid of catching cold; but I am told it lasted till about half past eleven. I have conversed with a person who saw it at a place about 30 miles north from this city. There it had the same appearance and seemed to pass through the zenith. I have written to Philadelphia to know whether it was seen there but have not yet received an answer. The day following was very hot. Monday morning was overcast, but sultry. About 2 o'clock the sun broke out, and it seemed as if we should have a very hot day, but about noon there arose a dark, smoky vapor which covered the whole heavens, sometimes so thick as to quite hide the sun, sometimes only obscuring it so as to make it appear like a great ball of fire, or a dark red full moon. This smoky vapor lasted the whole day, and in the evening, there was a smell very much like that form burning green brush wood. Next day the vapor continued, but in a much less degree. Since that we have had two thunder gusts, which have cleared the air, and the northern lights have disappeared.[6]

In the same letter, Thomson inquired of Jefferson what would be the probable effects of a sudden change of the earth's position, say, for

---

6. Collections of the New York Historical Society for the year 1878, p. 212.

instance, by an alteration of the poles and inclination of the axis 23½ degrees, or a change in the annual orbit. This question led Jefferson to write a lengthy dissertation on the structure of the globe, in which he said:

> The Creator, therefore, of a revolving solid would make it an
> oblate spheroid, that figure alone admitting a perfect equilibrium.
> He would make it in that form for another reason; that is, to
> prevent a shifting of the axis of rotation. Had he created the earth
> perfectly spherical, its axis might have been perpetually shifting
> by the influence of the other bodies of the system, and by placing
> the inhabitants of the earth successively under its poles, it might
> have been depopulated; whereas being spheroidical, it has but
> one axis on which it can revolve in equilibrium. Suppose the axis
> of the earth to shift 45 degrees, then cut it in 180 slices, making
> every section in the plane of a circle of latitude perpendicular to
> the axis: every one of these slices, except the equatorial one, would
> be unbalanced, as there would be more matter on one side of its
> ais than on the other. There could be but one diameter drawn
> through such a slice which would divide it into two equal parts;
> on every other possible diameter the parts would hang unequal;
> this would produce an irregularity in the diurnal rotation. We
> may, therefore, conclude it impossible for the poles of the earth
> to shift if it was made spheroidically, and that it would be made
> spheroidical, though solid, to obtain this end. I use this reasoning
> only on the supposition that the earth has had a beginning.

The two philosophers next enter upon a discussion of rock formations, Thomson writing to Jefferson in April 1787, for an explanation of the horizontal strata in our western country. With his unusual readiness to treat scientific subjects, Jefferson at once replied:

> With respect to the inclination of the strata of rocks, I had
> observed them between the Blue Ridge and North Mountain,
> in Virginia, to be parallel with the pole of the earth. I observed

the same thing, in most instances, in the Alps, between Nice and Turin, but, in returning along the precipices of the Apennines, where they hang over the Mediterranean, their direction was totally different and various, and you mention that in our western country they are horizontal. This variety proves that they have not been formed by subsidence as some writers of the theories of the earth have pretended – for then they should always have been in circular strata and concentric. It proves, too, that they have not been formed by the rotation of the earth on its axis, as might have been suspected had all these strata been parallel with that axis. They may, indeed, have been thrown up by explosions, as Whitehurst supposes, or have been the effect of convulsions. But there can be no proof of their explosion, nor is it probable that convulsions have deformed every spot of the earth; it is now generally believed that rock grows, and it seems that it grows in layers in every direction, as the branches of trees grow in all directions, they seek further the solution of this phenomenon.

In 1787, Jefferson published a book entitled *Notes on the State of Virginia*, the manuscript having first been submitted to Thomson for his criticisms. Thomson added several observations, which Jefferson considered so valuable that he placed them in the volume as an appendix. Thomson first called attention to two channels of communication between the western waters and the Atlantic, of particular interest to Pennsylvanians: "one from Presque Isle, on Lake Erie to Le Bœuf, down the Allegheny to Kiskiminitas, then up the Kiskiminitas, and from thence a small portage to Juniata, which flows into the Susquehanna; the other from Lake Ontario, to the east branch of the Delaware, and down to Philadelphia." He regarded these two routes as practicable, and he predicted that both of them would be opened and improved.[7]

Thomson's observations on the geological formation of the Blue Ridge Mountains and the Atlantic slope are written in beautiful language

---

7. Notes on the State of Virginia, p. 333; also see The Westward Movement by Justin Winsor, p. 250.

and the true scientific spirit. His remarks on this subject indicate an extraordinary familiarity with the history of the globe, and on this account, they are given in full:

> The reflections I was led into on viewing this passage of the
> Potomac through the Blue Ridge were, that this country must
> have suffered some violent convulsion, and that the face of
> it must have been changed from what it probably was some
> centuries ago: that the broken and ragged faces of the mountains
> on each side of the river; the tremendous rocks, which are left
> with one end fixed in the precipice, and the other jutting out,
> and seemingly ready to fall for want of support; the bed of the
> river for several miles below obstructed, and filled with the loose
> stones carried from this mound; in short, everything on which
> you cast your eye evidently demonstrates a disrupture and breach
> in the mountain, and that, before this happened, what is now
> a fruitful vale, was formerly a great lake or collection of water,
> which possibly might have here formed a mighty cascade, or
> had its vent to the ocean by the Susquehanna, where the Blue
> Ridge seems to terminate. Besides this, there are other parts of
> the country which bear evident traces of a like convulsion. From
> the best accounts I have been able to obtain, the place where the
> Delaware now flows through the Kittatinny Mountain, which is
> a continuation of what is called the North Ridge, or Mountain,
> was not its original course, but that it passed through what is now
> called 'the Wind-gap,' a place several miles to the westward, and
> above a hundred feet higher than the present bed of the river. The
> Wind-gap is about a mild broad, and the stones in it such as seem
> to have been washed for ages by water running over them. Should
> this have been the case, there must have been a large lake behind
> that mountain, and by some uncommon swell in the waters,
> or by some convulsion of nature, the river must have opened
> its way through a different part of the mountain, and meeting
> there with less obstruction, carried away with it the opposing

mounds of earth, deluged the country below with the immense
collection of waters to which this new passage gave vent. There
are still remaining, and daily discovered, innumerable instances
of such a deluge on both sides of the river, after it passed the hills
above the falls of Trenton and reached the champaign. On the
New Jersey side, which is flatter that the Pennsylvania side, all the
country below Croswick hills seems to have been overflowed to
the distance of from ten to fifteen miles back from the river, and
to have acquired new soil by the earth and clay brought down
and mixed with the native sand. The spot on which Philadelphia
stands evidently appears to be made ground. The different strata
through which they pass in digging to water, the acorns, leaves,
and sometimes branches, which are found twenty feet below the
surface, all seem to demonstrate this. I am informed that at Yor-
ktown, in Virginia, in the bank of York river, there are different
strata of shells and earth, one above another, which seem to point
out that the country there has undergone several changes; that
the sea has, for a succession of ages, occupied the place where dry
land now appears; and that the ground has been suddenly raised
at various periods. What a change would it make in the country
below, should the mountains at Niagara, by an accident, be cleft
asunder, and a passage suddenly opened to drain off the waters of
Erie and the Upper lakes! While ruminating on these subjects, I
have often been hurried away by fancy, and led to imagine, that
what is now the bay of Mexico, was once a champaign country;
and that from the point or cape of Florida, there was a continued
range of mountains through Cuba, Hispaniola, Porto Rico,
Martinique, Guadeloupe, Barbados, and Trinidad, till it reached
the shores of America, and formed the shores which bounded the
ocean, and guarded the country behind: that, by some convulsion
or shock of nature, the sea had broken through these mounts,
and deluged that vast plain, till it reached the foot of the Andes;
that being there heaped up by the trade winds, always blowing
from one quarter, it had found its way back, as it continues to

do, through the gulf between Florida and Cuba, carrying with it the loam and sand it may have scooped from the country it had occupied, part of which it may have deposited on the shores of North America, and with part formed the Banks of Newfoundland. – But these are only the visions of fancy.[8]

The remainder of Thomson's observations refer principally to the habits and characteristics of the North American Indians, a subject with which he was thoroughly familiar. It is gratifying to reflect upon the deep interest that our early statesmen took in scientific and literary subjects. The cares of state were lightened by the consolations of learning, and political disappointments were forgotten in a communication between kindred minds. Thomson found much happiness in these pursuits, and his abilities were recognized by various learned societies the degree of L.L.D. from the University of Pennsylvania in 1784 and Princeton College in 1822.

8. Notes on the State of Virginia, p 334.

American Philosophical Society Philadelphia

Thomas Jefferson

Portrait of Lafayette

chapter eight

*Literary Pursuits—The
Septuagint—Translation of the Bible
from the Greek—Synopsis of the
Four Evangelists*

In peaceful retirement at Harriton,[1] the most interesting character in Thomson's life begins. Although he had written many letters and papers of great historical value during his public career, it was a period of literary activity and scholarly pursuits. Long before this, in 1759, his interest in Indian affairs prompted him to write the *Enquiry into the Causes of the Alienation of the Delaware and Shawenese Indians from the British Interest*, an account of which is given in Chapter III. As early as 1783, John Jay had urged him to write a history of the Revolution, marking at the time:

> When I consider that no person in the world is so perfectly acquainted with the rise, conduct, and conclusion of the American Revolution as yourself, I cannot but wish that you would devote one hour in the four and twenty to giving comprised in a small compass. It need not be burdened with *minute* accounts of

---

1. For an account on the estate at Harriton, see Chapter IX.

Battles, Retreats, Evacuations, etc.; leave those matters to voluminous historians. The political history of the Revolution will be
most liable to misrepresentation, and future relations of it will
probably be replete both with intentional and accidental errors.
Such a work would be highly important to the Cause of Truth
with posterity. I don't mean that it should be published during
your life, that would be improper for many reasons; nor do I
think it should be known that you was employed in such a work.[2]

Dr. Ramsay, in 1809, confirmed this idea, and encouraged him to
write the history, adding: "I suppose that your modesty has restrained
you from doing justice to yourself in many services you have rendered
the memorable cause of American liberty."

It is said that Thomson actually began to collect materials for such
a history and that after writing many pages, he resolved to destroy the
whole. He gave as his reason for this action, that to make the work impartial, it would be necessary to blur the reputation of many prominent
families, and this he was unwilling to do. Some authorities claim that
these papers were not destroyed until after Thomson had removed to
Harriton, but Winthrop Sargent, editor of the *Loyalist Versus of Stansbury
and Odell*,[3] intimates that it took place as early as 1779. On September
18th of this year, the following lines from "The Word of Congress," written by Jonathan Odell, appeared in *Rivington's Gazette*,

Have you not read the marvelous escapes,
Of Proteus shifting to a thousand shapes;
Have you not seen the wonders of the stage?
When pantomime delights a trifling age;

---

2. Collections of the New York Historical Society for the year 1878, p. 174.

3. Joseph Stansbury was a native of England and settled in Philadelphia a few years before the Revolution. He was a man of literary tastes. In 1776, it was reported that he sang "God Save the King" in his
house and that a number of persons present bore him chorus. Before the close of the year, he was committed to prison on account of his loyalist sentiments. In 1777, he was released, and received an appointment
from Sir William Howe. In 1780 his property was confiscated, after which he removed to New York, where
he died in 1809.

Such and more various, such and more absurd,
Charles Thomson witness of the changeful word,
He'll sign to anything, no matter what—
At truth alone, his pen would make a blot."

Sargent claims that the poet, in the last two lines, was referring to Thomson's unwillingness to tell the truth about some of the Revolutionary characters. Whatever the cause that inspired him to destroy his papers, history's loss was an irreparable one. Many transactions of the old Congress and the motives that swayed its members remain obscure.[4]

In the year 1808, Thomson gave the world the first American translation of the Septuagint into English. From his boyhood, he had been a careful student of the Bible, while his love for Greek began in Dr. Alison's school in New London. John F. Watson gives the following account of how Thomson's interest in the Septuagint was first awakened:

His first passion for Greek literature was induced, as he told me, by a seeming accident. Passing an auction store, he heard the crier proclaiming the sale of an 'unknown, outlandish book;' he bid a trifle for it and got it. It proved to be a part of the Greek Septuagint. When he had mastered it enough to understand it, his anxiety was extreme to see the whole; but he could find no copy, until, strange to tell, in the interval of two years, passing the same store and looking in, he actually saw the remainder selling off, when he joyfully bought it at a few pence. I used to tell him the 'Translation,' which he made from that copy (the first, I believe in the English language), should have been furnished with the story as a proper subject for its *preface*. For this great work, on which he occupied himself so many years, is strangely enough without introduction or advertisement to the reader. It wanted

---

4. Charles Thomson, the patriotic Secretary of the Old Congress, wrote its history, which he intended to publish; but his courage failed at the pinch, and he burnt it. We might guess his reasons, even if he had not given them, when we read the "Diary of John Adams." John Adams and Other Essays, by Mellen Chamberlain. P 272.

something of the kind and a hint to the common English reader
that it was a book of great authority in biblical elucidation. His
modesty kept him from giving any preface; and being offered
for sale without any published commendations from others,
it did not receive its need of praise, nor its proper pecuniary
reimbursement.[5]

Some writers claim that the New Testament itself was Thomson's
inspiring motive to translate the Septuagint into English. Mr. Albert J.
Edmunds, of the Historical Society of Pennsylvania, calls attention to
a fragment in Thomson's handwriting which reads as follows: "As the
quotations which the writers of the New Testament made from the Old,
either to show the predictions of the prophets are fulfilled in Jesus Christ,
or to confirm and enforce the doctrines they delivered, or convey their
own thoughts on different subjects, are chiefly taken from the Septuagint; and as, upon inquiry, I could not find that there was any translation
of this into English, . . ."[6]

No doubt, Thomson was led to translating the Septuagint primarily
on account of the many quotations from it in the New Testament. This
seems to accord with the view of Dr. Adam Clarke, who said: "No man
can adequately understand the New Testament Scriptures who has not
diligently read the Septuagint."

It may seem strange that the Septuagint's value was first properly
appreciated in this country by a layman. This version of the Scriptures
is of great importance to all students, of Biblical literature, as the oldest translation of considerable extent that was ever written; as the only
independent witness for the text of the Old Testament, and as the basis
of so many passages in the New Testament. Thomson was a man of truth
in all things, and he sought to give a just interpretation of the Scriptures.
On January 6, 1801, he wrote to Rev. Samuel Miller: "It has occupied
my closest attention and been my constant study and employment for
more than twelve years. Attached to no system nor peculiar tenets of

---

5. Annals of Philadelphia and Pennsylvania, Vol. I, p. 568.
6. Pennsylvania Magazine of History and Biography, Vol. 15, p. 329.

any sect or party, I have sought for truth with the utmost ingenuity, and endeavored to give a just and true representation of the sense and meaning of the Sacred Scriptures; and in doing this, I have further endeavored to convey into the translation, as far as I could, the spirit and manner of the authors, and thereby give it the quality of an original."

In the history of the Scriptures, the country seat at Harriton deserves to be mentioned with Alexandria. Much prominence is given to the legend connected with the writing of the Septuagint. Demetrius Phalerus, the Alexandrian library's keeper, proposed to King Ptolemy II to have a Greek translation of the Jewish law made for the library. The King consented and appointed an embassy to the high priest, Eleazar, at Jerusalem, requesting him to send six ancient, worthy, and learned men from each of the twelve tribes to translate the law for him at Alexandria. Eleazar at once consented and sent the seventy-two men with a precious roll of the law. They were received with great honor at the Alexandria court and conducted to the Island Pharos, where they might work undisturbed and isolated. When they had agreed upon a section, Demetrius wrote down their version; the whole translation was finished in seventy-two days. The Jewish community of Alexandria was allowed to have a copy and accepted the version officially, a curse being laid upon introducing any changes. Such is the legend. The truth is that the work of translation went on gradually. In 130 B.C., not only the law but the prophets also were extant in Greek, and as new books were added, the scope of the Greek Bible was greatly enlarged. How different is this legend from the simple story of the first American translation of the Septuagint into English! A modest patriot of the Revolution, Thomson, saw his country safely through the perils of war and then retired to give his days and nights to his favorite study. Without prejudice or the bias of sect, he proceeded to his task, seeking not to establish theories but to find the truth.

It appears that Thomson began work on the translations early in the year 1789 and that he was almost continuously employed in it until 1808. In 1801, he wrote to Rev. Samuel Miller: "I have made four copies of the whole Bible, and of some books the fifth copy, and am now making a fifth copy of the whole."

In 1808, the year that the translation was published, Thomson wrote to Jefferson: "I am truly thankful to that kind Providence, which directed my attention to this work. It has kept my mind employed, so that I can say I have not during the last nine years found one hour hang heavy on me."

The translation was issued in four octavo volumes, with the following title page: "The Holy Bible, containing the Old and New Covenant, commonly called the Old and New Testament: Translated from Greek. By Charles Thomson, Late Secretary to the Congress of the United States, Philadelphia: Printed by Jane Aitken.[7] No. 71 North Third Street, 1808, 4 vols."

Jefferson was very much interested in the translation, and he wrote to Thomson in January 1808, making several suggestions regarding the proper size of the volumes: "I see by the newspapers your translation of the Septuagint is now to be printed, and I write this to pray to be admitted as a subscriber. I wish it may not be too late for you to reconsider the size in which it is to be published. Folios and quartos are now laid aside because of their inconvenience. Everything is now printed in 8vo, 12mo, or petit format. The English booksellers print their first editions indeed in 4vo, because they can assess a larger price on account of the novelty; but the bulk of readers generally wait for the second edition, which is for the most part in 8vo. This is what I have long practiced myself. Johnson, of Philadelphia, set the example of printing handsome editions of the Bible in 4 vols, 8 vo. I wish yours were in the same form."

The convenient octavo form in which the Bible appeared indicates that Thomson followed the suggestions of Jefferson. Thomson and Ebenezer Hazard assumed the expense of publication in partnership, but the enterprise failed to be profitable. Hazard afterward bought the edition, and it was stored in his garret for years. After his death, it was sold

---

7. The Aitkens were prominent publishes in Philadelphia. Robert Aitken was born at Dal Keith, Scotland, and served a regular apprenticeship with a bookbinder in Edinburgh. He came to Philadelphia as a bookseller in 1769; returned to Scotland the same year, and in 1771, again located in Philadelphia, and followed by the business of bookselling and bind. In 1774 he became a printer. In 1775, he published a magazine, and in 1782, an edition of the Bible claimed to be the first edition printed in America. He died in 1802, and his daughter, Jane Aitken, continued the business.

for wastepaper to Dr. Earles, a bookseller, at the corner of Fourth and Chestnut streets; so that nearly all the volumes were destroyed.

Before taking up a critical study of Thomson's Bible, it may be interesting to refer to his notes on his translation, which have been preserved. The manuscript of the Septuagint is in the Library of Allegheny College, presented to that institution in 1825, by a nephew, John Thomson. Thomson's copy of the Septuagint is in the Ridgeway branch of the Philadelphia Library. It contains numerous corrections and revisions, showing that interest in his favorite study was maintained until the time of his death. About twenty-five years ago, three manuscripts relating to the translation were discovered in a junk shop in Philadelphia. They were at once purchased by the Historical Society of Pennsylvania and were deposited in the library. The first manuscript is a rough notebook containing discussions about the meaning of certain Greek words, etc. The second manuscript is a complete copy of the New Testament, inscribed with the words, "Not a correct copy." The third manuscript also contains the whole New Testament, but it was not the copy used by the printers as it varies slightly from the published edition.[8] This verifies the remark made by Thomson to Rev. Samuel Miller, "I have made four copies of the whole Bible, and of some books the fifth copy."

The copy of the Septuagint used by Thomson in doing the translation was I. Field's duodecimo, printed at Cambridge in 1665. At the beginning of his notebook, Thomson gives some rules which the translator should faithfully observe. He says: "To translate well is: 1, to give a just representation of the purpose of an author; 2, to convey into the translation the author's spirit and manner; 3, to give it the quality of an original by making it appear natural, a natural copy without applying words improperly, or in a meaning not warranted by use, or combining them in a way which renders the sense obscure, and the construction ungrammatical or harsh."

Several examples will now be given comparing Thomson's Bible with the Authorized Version and the Revised Version of 1881-1885.

---

8. Pennsylvania Magazine of History and Biography, Vol. 15, p. 331.

(GENESIS 1:1-5.)

Authorized Version.	Thomson's Translation.	Revised Version of 1881-1885.
In the beginning God created the heaven and the earth. ² And the earth was without form, and void; and darkness was upon the face of the deep. And the Spirit of God moved upon the face of the waters. ³ And God said, Let there be light; and there was light. ⁴ And God saw the light, that it was good; and God divided the light from the darkness. ⁵ And God called the light Day, and the darkness he called Night. And the evening and the morning were the first day.	In the beginning, God created the heaven and the earth. And the earth was invisible and unfurnished, and there was darkness over this abyss, and a breath of God was brought on above the water. And God said, "Let there be light;" and there was light. And God saw the light that it was good. And God made a separation between light and darkness. And God called the light Day; and darkness he called Night. And there was an evening and there was a morning. The first day.	¹ In the beginning God created the heaven and ² the earth. And the earth was waste and void; and darkness was upon the face of the deep; and the spirit of God moved upon the face of the waters. ³ And God said, Let there be light: and ⁴ there was light. And God saw the light, that it was good; and God divided the light from the darkness. ⁵ And God called the light Day, and the darkness he called Night. And there was evening and there was morning, one day.

Thomson's rendition of David's funeral ode over Saul and Jonathan is one of the most beautiful portions of the Bible, and it is given in comparison with the other versions:

(II Samuel 1:17-27.)

Authorized Version.	Thomson's Translation.
[17] And David lamented with this lamentation over Saul and over Jonathan his son: [18] (Also he bade them teach the children of Judah *the use of* the bow; behold, *it is* written in the book of Jasher.) [19] The beauty of Israel is slain upon they high places; how are the mighty fallen! [20] Tell *it* not in Gath, publish *it* not in the streets of Askelon; less the daughters of the Philistines rejoice, lest the daughters of the uncircumcised triumph. [21] Ye mountains of Gilboa, *let there be* no dew, neither *let there be* rain, upon you, nor fields of offerings; for there the shield of the mighty is vilely cast away, the shield of Saul, *as though he had not been* anointed with oil. [22] From the blood of the slain, from the fat of the mighty, the bow of Jonathan turned not back, and the sword of Saul returned not empty. [23] Saul and Jonathan *were* lovely and pleasant in their lives, and in their death, they were not divided; they were swifter than eagles, they were stronger than lions. [24] Ye daughters of Israel, weep over Saul, who clothed you in scarlet, with *other* delights, who put on ornaments of gold upon your apparel. [25] How are the mighty fallen in the midst of the battle! O Jonathan, *thou wast* slain in thine high places. [26] I am distressed for thee, my brother Jonathan; very pleasant hast thou been unto me; thy love to me was wonderful, passing the love of women. [27] How are the mighty fallen and the weapons of war perished!.	Then David sung this funeral Ode over Saul and over Jonathan his son and gave orders that the children of Juda should learn it. Behold it is written in the book *Straight*. Erect, O Israel, a monument for the dead— For the slain on thy lofty mountains. How are the mighty fallen! Proclaim not ye the news in Geth— Tell it not as good news in the streets of Ascalon; Lest the daughters of the Philistines rejoice— Lest the daughters of the uncircumcised exalt with joy. On you, mountains of Gelbua, let not dew descend— On you, let there be no rain, nor fields of first fruit offerings! For there the shield of the mighty was battered— The shield of Saul. Was he not anointed with oil? From the blood of the wounded - From the fat of the mighty, The bow of Jonathan recoiled not empty— The sword of Saul bended not in vain. Saul and Jonathan were beloved— They were lovely and inseparable; Comely in their life— And in their death, they were not divided. Than eagles they were swifter— And than lions more courageous. O daughters of Israel, weep for Saul, Who adorned your dress with scarlet— Who put ornaments of gold on your apparel. How are the mighty fallen! In the midst of battle, Jonathan! On thy lofty mountains slain! I mourn for thee, my brother Jonathan, To thee thou wast very lovely, Thy love for me was wonderful— Far surpassing the love of woman, How are the mighty fallen! And the weapons of war perished!

Revised Version of 1881-1885.

17 And David lamented with this lamentation over Saul and over

18 Jonathan his son: and he bade them teach the children of Judah *the song of* the bow: behold it is written in the book of Jashar.

19 Thy glory, O Israel, is slain upon thy high places! How are the mighty fallen!

20 Tell it not in Gath, Publish it not in the streets of Ashkelon; Lest the daughters of the Philistines rejoice,
Lest the daughters of the uncircumcised triumph.

21 Ye mountains of Gilboa, Let there be no dew nor rain upon you, neither fields of offerings:
For there the shield of the mighty was vilely cast away.
The shield of Saul now anointed with oil.

22 From the blood of the slain, from the fat of the mighty.
The bow of Jonathan turned not back,
And the sword of Saul returned not empty.

23 Saul and Jonathan were lovely and pleasant in their lives,
And in their death they were not divided:
They were swifter than eagles,
They were stronger than lions.

24 Ye daughters of Israel, weep over Saul,
Who clothed you in scarlet delicately,
Who put ornaments of gold upon your apparel.

25 How are the mighty fallen in the midst of the battle!
Jonathan is slain upon the high places.

26 I am distressed for thee, my brother Jonathan:
Very pleasant has thou been unto me:
Thy love to me was wonderful,
Passing the love of women.

27 How are the mighty fallen,
And the weapons of war perished!

It is quite evident that Thomson aimed, at all times, to transfer the thought of the Greek into expressive English. His translation may lack rhythm, but it cannot be surpassed in clearness, accuracy, and force. This is shown in the two psalms which follow:

(PSALM 1.)

Authorized Version.	Thomson's Translation.	Revised Version of 1881-1885.
BLESSED is the man that walketh not in the counsel of the ungodly, nor standeth in the way of sinners, nor sitteth in the seat of the of the scornful. ² But his delight is in the law of the LORD; and in his law doth he meditate day and night. ³ And he shall be like a tree planted by the rivers of water, that bringeth forth his fruit in his season; his leaf also shall not wither; and whatsoever he doeth shall prosper. ⁴ The ungodly are not so, but are like the chaff which the wind driveth away. ⁵ Therefore the ungodly shall not stand in the judgment, nor sinners in the congregation of the righteous. ⁶ For the LORD knoweth the way of the righteous; but the way of the ungodly shall perish.	HAPPY the man who hath not walked by the counsel of the wicked; nor stood in the way of sinners; nor sat in the seat of the scornful. His delight will be in the law of the Lord only. And on his law he will meditate day and night. And he will be like the tree planted by the streams of water, which will yield its fruit, in due season, and its leaf shall not fall untimely. In all that he doth he shall be prospered. Not so the wicked; not so. They are like the chaff, which the wind driveth from the face of the earth. Therefore the wicked shall not stand in judgment, nor sinners in the counsel of the righteous. For the Lord knoweth the way of the righteous: and the way of the ungodly shall perish.	¹ BLESSED is the man that walketh not in the counsel of the wicked, Nor standeth in the way of sinners. Nor sitteth in the seat of the scornful. ² But his delight is the law of the LORD; And in his law doth he meditate day and night. ³ And he shall be like a tree planted by the streams of water. That bringeth forth its fruit in its season, Whose leaf also doth not wither; And whatsoever he doeth shall prosper. ⁴ The wicked are not so; But are like the chaff which the wind driveth away. ⁵ Therefore the wicked shall not stand in the judgment, Nor sinners in the congregation of the righteous. ⁶ For the LORD knoweth the way of the righteous; But the way of the wicked shall perish.

(PSALM XXIII.)

Authorized Version.	Thomson's Translation.	Revised Version of 1881-1885.
The LORD *is* my shepherd; I shall not want. ² He maketh me to lie down in green pastures; he leadeth me beside the still waters. ³ He restoreth my soul: he leadeth me in the paths of righteousness for his name's sake. ⁴ Yea, though I walk through the valley of the shadow of death, I will fear no evil: for thou art with me: thy rod and thy staff they comfort me. ⁵ Thou preparest a table before me in the presence of mine enemies: thou anointest my head with oil; my cup runneth over. ⁶ Surely goodness and mercy shall follow me all the days of my life; and I will dwell in the house of the LORD forever.	The LORD is my shepherd. I shall want nothing. In a verdant pasture he hath fixed my abode. He hath led me by gently flowing water and restored my soul. He hath led me in the paths of righteousness for his name's sake. For though I walk amidst the shades of death, I will fear no ills, because thou art with me; thy rod and thy staff have been my comfort. Thou hast spread a table before me; in the presence of them who afflict me. With oil thou hast anointed my head; and thine exhilarating cup is the very best. Thy mercy will surely follow me all the days of my life; and my dwelling shall be in the house of the Lord to the length of days.	¹ The LORD is my shepherd; I shall not want. ² He maketh me to lie down in green pastures; He leadeth me beside the still waters. ³ He restoreth my soul: He guides me in the paths of righteousness for his name's sake. ⁴ Yea, though I walk through the valley of the shadow of death, I will fear no evil; for thou art with me: Thy rod and thy staff they comfort me. ⁵ Thou preparest a table before me in the presence of mine enemies; Thou has anointed my head with oil; my cup runneth over. ⁶ Surely goodness and mercy shall follow me all the days of my life; And I will dwell in the house of the LORD for ever.

The same peculiar interest attends the study of the New Testament translation; indeed, it seems that this part of Thomson's work surpasses the Old Testament in clearness and felicity of language. He opens the first chapter of Matthew as follows: "*The Genealogy of Jesus Christ, son of David, son of Abraham.* Abraham begat Isaac, and Isaac begat Jacob, etc."

In his copy of the Bible, he afterward changed this to read: "A roll of genealogy of Jesus Christ, a son [that is] a descendant of David, a descendent of Abraham. Abraham was the father of Isaac, and Isaac was the father of Jacob," etc.

His notebook on the New Testament is of the rarest value as a commentary on the Scriptures. His rendition of certain passages will now be given, followed by the discussions as found in the notebook:

(MATTHEW XII: 31-32.)

Authorized Version.	Thomson's Translation.	Revised Version of 1881-1885.
[31] Wherefore I say unto you, All manner of sin and blasphemy shall be forgiven unto men; but the blasphemy *against* the *Holy Ghost* shall not be forgiven unto men. [32] And whosoever speaketh a word against the Son of man, it shall be forgiven him, but whosoever speaketh against the Holy Ghost, it shall not be forgiven him, neither in this world, neither in the world to come.	Therefore I say to you, All manner of sin and slander may be forgiven men; but this slanderous speaking against the spirit is not to be forgiven men—Even though one speak against the Son of man, it may be forgiven him; but whoever shall speak against the Holy Spirit is not to be forgiven; either in the present age, or in that to come.	[31] Therefore I say unto you, Every sin and blasphemy shall be forgiven unto men; but the blasphemy against the Spirit shall [32] not be forgiven. And whoever shall speak a word against the Son of man, it shall be forgiven him; but whosoever shall speak against the Holy Spirit, it shall not be forgiven him, neither in this world, nor in [33] that which is to come.

Referring to this passage in his notebook under the heading, "*Aiōn,*" Thomson says: "A true knowledge of what I am inclined to think is the scriptural meaning of this, would have removed all difficulty from a text of scripture which has given much trouble to many weak Christians."

He also suggests that the passage may be translated: "Neither under the present dispensation, namely the Mosaical, nor under the coming, namely the Christian," adding that the word at times seems to signify a state or dispensation, sometimes a period of long duration or eternity. The notebook contains an interesting comment on the phrase "hardness of heart," found in the New Testament. "Hardness of heart or hardheartedness," the translator says, "does not mean inhumanity, which is the import of the English word; but stubbornness, or an intractable temper. The reason of this diversity in the etymology seems to arise from this: that among the Greeks and Romans, the heart was supposed to be the seat of wisdom, intelligence, or understanding; among the English, that of courage or affection; and hence among the Greeks, the phrase "to harden the heart' meant to render it indocile, intractable, stubborn and contumacious. In the same manner among the Greeks and Romans, the spleen was accounted the seat of mirth and laughter, but among the English, that of ill-humor and melancholy."

The familiar words of John on the necessity of regeneration are now given in the three translations for comparison:

(JOHN III: 7-8.)

Authorized Version.	Thomson's Translation.	Revised Version of 1881-1885.
[7] Marvel not that I said unto thee, Ye must be born again. [8] The wind bloweth where it listeth, and thou hearest the sound thereof, but canst not tell whence it cometh, and whither it goeth; so is every one that is born of the Spirit.	Wonder not at my telling thee, You must be born again. That blast of wind bloweth where it pleaseth, and thou hearest the sound of it, but dost know whence it cometh and whither it goeth. So is every one that is born of the spirit.	[7] Marvel not that I said unto thee, Ye must be [8] born anew. The wind bloweth where it listeth, and thou hearest the voice thereof, but knowest not whence it cometh, and whether it goeth: so is every one that is born [9] of the Spirit.

In this passage, the notebook is rich in suggestions. Thomson doubted the propriety of the common translation, "the wind bloweth where it listeth." At the same time, he defended his view as follows:

John had said 'unless a man be born again, he cannot see the kingdom of God." Nicodemus apprehending that he spoke of a second natural generation and birth, asked with surprise, how this could be. Jesus corrects his mistake by telling him that unless a man be born of water and spirit, he cannot see the kingdom of God, and then proceeds to explain himself farther by telling him that what is born of the flesh is flesh, and what is born of the spirit is spirit; therefore, he should not be surprised at his telling him that he must be born again. I am, therefore, inclined to think he is directing the attention of Nicodemus to the spirit mentioned before, and that it should be translated as I have done, and that the sound of it refers to what Nicodemus had said, 'None can do the miracles which thou dost.' Upon farther consideration, I am of the opinion that it refers to a sudden blast of wind, and that it is mentioned to show that there are things in the natural world, as well as in the supernatural which we must believe though we cannot account for them.

Critical scholars on both continents favorably received Thomson's version of the Scriptures. The American revisers of the Bible frequently consulted it, and in many cases, he anticipates the Revised Version of 1881. Orme wrote of it in 1824: "This transatlantic work is creditable to America and to the learned author. It is the only English version of the Septuagint, and is therefore worthy of attention, as well as for the fidelity with which it is executed. The New Testament contains many improved renderings and improvements."[9]

Horne likewise commended the translation in the highest terms. In his *Manual of Biblical Bibliography*, published in 1839, appears the following notice: "This translation is, upon the whole, faithfully executed, though that of the Old Testament, being a version of a version, can hardly afford much assistance to the biblical student. The New Testament translation is much improved in the punctuation and in the arrangement of the objections and replies that occasion such frequent transitions in St. Paul's Epistles. The notes which accompany this work are brief but satisfactory as far as they go."[10]

The most accurate estimate of Thomson's work is probably given by Dr. Francis Bowen, of Harvard College. "This solitary and unaided

---

9. Bibliotheca Biblica, p 429
10. Manual of Biblical Bibliography, p. 263.

scholar, over three quarters of a century ago [writes Dr. Bowen], living in what might have been viewed from the English standpoint as a small provincial city, having at his disposal none of the rich means and appliances of scholarship which were collected in the Jerusalem chamber of Westminster Abbey, and in fact probably possessing hardly any books available for his purpose except an English Bible and a copy of the Textus Receptus of the Greek New Testament and Septuagint, has yet produced a work which may well challenge comparison with the best results of the united labors, during the last ten years, of two companies containing thirty or forty of the best scholars in England and America."

In 1815, Thomson's *Harmony of the Four Gospels* appeared, having the title page, "A Synopsis of the Four Evangelists; by Charles Thomson, Philadelphia: Published for the Author, William McCulloch, Printer, 1815."

Thomson considered the Gospels as a series of memoirs of the important sayings and events in Christ's life. He arranged all such passages according to the dates, places, and circumstances, employing a literal translation of the evangelists' very words. Considerable importance is attached to this work on account of the correspondence that it stimulated with Jefferson. In 1816, the Sage of Monticello wrote to Thomson:

This work bears the stamp of that accuracy which marks everything from you, and will be useful to them who, not taking things on trust, read for themselves to the fountain of pure morals. I too have made a wee title book from the same materials which I call the 'Philosophy of Jesus.' It is a paradigma of his doctrines, made by cutting the texts out of the book and arranging them on pages of a blank book, in a certain order of time or subject. A more beautiful or precious morsel of this I have never seen. It is a document in proof that I am a real Christian, that is to say, a disciple of the doctrines of Jesus, very different from the Platonists who call me infidel and themselves Christians; and preachers of the gospel, while they draw all their characteristic dogmas from what its author never said or saw, they have compounded from the heathen mysteries a system beyond the comprehension of man of which the great reformer of the vicious ethics and deism of the Jews, were he to return on the earth, would not recognize one feature.

In the closing years of his life, Jefferson, like Thomson, spent much time meditating upon the subject of Christianity. In 1803, he compared the merits of Jesus with those of others, embracing a comparative view of the ethics of Christianity, Judaism, and ancient philosophy. He was so impressed with the doctrine of Christianity that he declared: "Its author had presented to the world a system of morals, which, if filled up in the style and spirit of the rich fragments he has left us, would be the most perfect and sublime that has ever been taught by man."

The correspondence between Jefferson and Thomson on this subject shows, in a clear light, the religious side of their nature. Thomson had been an elder in the First Presbyterian Church, Philadelphia; but in 1801, he wrote, when speaking of the progress of his Bible translation, "Attached to no system nor peculiar tenets of any sect or party, I have sought for truth with the utmost ingenuity."

In 1803, Jefferson declared that his whole life had been devoted to an inquiry and reflection on the Christian religion. As a result, he found that Christ had "pushed his scrutinies into the heart of man, erected his tribunal in the region of his thoughts, and purified the waters at the fountain head."

It appears that Jefferson, in his *Philosophy of Jesus*, and Thomson, in his *Synopsis of the Four Evangelists*, were striving towards the same great end—to find the truth in its simplest form. Thomson frequently had his resentment stirred up by the charges of infidelity made against Jefferson, and he always defended his "ancient friend" by quoting his own words: "I, too, have made a wee little book from the same materials, which I call the 'Philosophy of Jesus.' . . . It is a document in proof that I am a real Christian."

Jefferson took a philosophical view of the matter and wrote to Thomson in January 1817:

Say nothing of my religion; it is known to myself and my God alone; its evidence before the world is to be sought in my life; if that has been honest and dutiful to society, the religion which has regulated it cannot be a bad one. It is a singular anxiety which some people have that we should all think alike. Would the world be more beautiful were all our faces alike? Were our tempers, our talents, our tastes, our forms, our wishes, aversions and pursuits cast exactly in the same mold? If no varieties existed in the animal, vegetable, or mineral creation, but all move strictly uniform, catholic and orthodox, what a world of physical and moral monotony would it be! These are the absurdities into which those run who usurp the throne of God and dictate to Him what He should have done. May they with all their metaphysical riddles appear before that tribunal with as clean hands and hearts as you and I shall. There, suspended in the scales of eternal justice, faith and works will show their worth by their weight.

Thomson's papers include a manuscript pamphlet entitled, "Critical Annotations on Gilbert Wakefield's Works."[11] This manuscript passed into the hands of John F. Watson, who, in 1832, presented it to the Massachusetts Historical Society. It is quite likely that Wakefield influenced Thomson in making his translation of the Bible. About 1780, Wakefield published a translation of Matthew and the first epistle to the Thessalonians, while in 1792, the first edition of his complete Bible appeared. He retained as much of the language of the authorized version as seemed consistent with accuracy. The work was very popular, and it soon reached a second edition.

---

11. Gilbert Wakefield was born at Nottingham, England, February 22, 1756. He was educated at Cambridge and became a fine classical scholar. He was ordained as a minister in the Church of England in 1778, but he left the church the following year to become a teacher. He won great reputation by his Bible translation. He afterwards became involved in political controversy, and for some imprudent remarks, he was arrested and sentenced to two years' imprisonment. He died in 1801.

Harriton House

chapter nine

Thomson's Family —
The Estate of Harriton

hus far, but slight reference has been made to Thomson's
domestic life. He was twice married, his first wife being Ruth, a
daughter of John Mather, of Chester, Pennsylvania. The Mathers
were among the earliest settlers in Penn's colony, Richard having arrived
at Philadelphia, October 31, 1685. John and James Mather were Chester
taxable as early as 1724, and it appears that they were men of great influence in their town. John married Mary Hoskins in 1730, and they had
three children, Joseph, Ruth, the wife of Charles Thomson, and Jane.
John Mather became a prosperous merchant, and he also served for a
time as Justice of the Common Pleas. He was prominent in church affairs, and in 1727 was elected warden in St. Paul's Episcopal Church,
Chester, while his name appears on the list of vestrymen as late as 1760.
He died in 1768, and the *Pennsylvania Gazette*, of November 17th that
year contained an obituary notice which reads thus:

> On Saturday last, departed this life, John Mather, Esq., an
> ancient inhabitant of Chester, in the 73d year of his age. During
> that long period, in every station of life in which he was placed,
> his Reputation for Piety, Honesty, and Benevolence was universal.

Stranger to civil and religious Rage,
The good man walked innoxious through his Age,
Unlearned, he knew no Schoolman's subtle Art,
No language but the language of the Heart,
By nature honest, by Experience wise,
Healthy by temperance, and by exercise.

Charles Thomson, his wife, and her sister, Jane Jackson, were named in the will as executors. The estate was considerable, including several houses and tracts of land in the vicinity of Chester; while on January 20, 1769, the following inventory of personal property was made:

	£	s.	d.
Wearing apparel	28	0	0
Bonds	956	19	0
Household furniture	277	14	6
Stock at Ridley	220	14	0
	1483	**7**	**6**

By the terms of the will, Thomson's wife received £200 and some real estate at Ridley, besides which she and her husband acquired a life estate in several valuable properties in Chester. Before this, in 1739, her grandmother, Ruth Hoskins, had devised to her the tavern in Chester, known as the Pennsylvania Arms. At this time, Thomson had considerable wealth of his own, having been successful in various business enterprises. His residence was at the corner of Spruce and Fourth streets, Philadelphia, one of the city's most attractive homes. His wife was a very amiable woman but was soon taken from him by death. By her, he had two children, twins, who died in infancy. As Thomson's wife left no issue, he released to Mary Jackson, John Mather's granddaughter, the properties in Chester, per the terms of Mather's will.

The circumstances of Thomson's second marriage in 1774 have already been related. The bride, Hannah Harrison, was the daughter of Richard Harrison, a wealthy Friend, of Maryland, who settled on the

"Welsh Tract," near Philadelphia, early in the eighteenth century. There is a fascinating history connected with this tract or "barony." Many of the Welsh Quakers, persuaded by the liberal promises made by William Penn, determined to settle in the province. However, before coming, a conference was held with Penn in 1681, when an agreement was made that the Welsh settlers' lands should be laid adjacent to each other. They were located on the watershed between Darby Creek and the Schuylkill River, on lands comprising the townships of Merion, Haverford, and Radnor. Holmes surveyed a tract of 40,000 acres under Penn's instructions, dated March 13, 1684. The region possessed many natural advantages and had an abundance of excellent streams, good timber, and fine building stone.[1] John Oldmixon, who visited the tract in 1708, says: "It is very populous, and the people very industrious; by which means this country is better cleared than any other part of the province. The inhabitants have many fine plantations of corn, and breed abundance of cattle; insomuch that they are looked upon to be as thriving and wealthy as any in the province—and this must always be said of the Welsh, that wherever they come, 'tis not their fault if they do not live, and live well too; for they seldom spare for labor, which seldom fails of success."

The object of the Welsh in desiring a separate barony was that they might have established liberty of worship and a government vested in persons elected by themselves. Authority for creating baronies and manors was granted to William Penn by the Charter from King Charles the Second, which provided: "And by these presents, we give and grant license unto the said William Penn, and his heirs, likewise to all and every such person and persons to whom the said William Penn, or his heirs shall at any time hereafter, grant any estate of inheritance as aforesaid, to erect any parcels of land within the province aforesaid, into manors, by and with the license to be first had and obtained for that purpose under the hand and seal of the said William Penn or his heirs, and in every of the said manors, to "have and hold a Court Baron, with all things whatsoever, which to a Court Baron do belong." [2]

---

1. Merion and the Welsh Tract by Glenn, p 25.
2. The Duke of Yorke's Book of Laws, p. 88.

The Welsh settlers planned to elect a certain number of justices, the Chief Justice to act as the Reeve of the Barony. These justices could determine all minor disputes, and they might levy taxes when approved by a vote of the people. The plan met with only partial success, and the barony soon became involved in many troubles, the first arising in 1687 over the boundaries of the tract. In 1688, the Welsh settlers refused to consider themselves included within the counties of Philadelphia and Chester. Therefore, they would not consent to bear any portion of the taxes or perform jury duty. They were not numerous enough to occupy the whole of the barony, and as they had refused to pay quit rents, their petition to be regarded as a manor was denied. As a result, the unsettled portions of the tract were soon granted to other purchasers.[3]

Rowland Ellis was one of the early Welsh settlers to locate upon this tract. He was born in North Wales in 1650, and, in 1686, he determined to visit Pennsylvania. Pleased with his observations, he returned home, and at once prepared to bring his family to America. They came to Pennsylvania in 1687 and settled at Bryn Mawr, on the "Welsh Tract," where Ellis took up a plantation of nearly seven hundred acres. He was a man of great natural ability and soon entered public life, representing Philadelphia County for a time in the General Assembly. He was a leading member of the Society of Friends and was also an able preacher.

In 1717, Richard Harrison, Jr., of Herring Creek, Western Shore of Maryland, came into the Province of Pennsylvania. During his stay, he married Hannah Norris, daughter of Isaac Norris, and granddaughter of Deputy-Governor Thomas Lloyd. It had been arranged before the marriage that Mrs. Harrison was to go into Maryland and that if, after residing there one year, she did not like it for a home, her husband would remove to Pennsylvania. In 1719, Richard Harrison returned to his wife's native land and purchased of Rowland Ellis his tract of seven hundred acres near Bryn Mawr.[4]

---

3. Shepherd's Proprietary Government in Pennsylvania, p. 46.
4. Pennsylvania Magazine of History and Biography, Vol. 13, p. 447; also, Collections of the Historical Society of Montgomery County, Pa., Vol. I, p. 396.

The house in which the Harrisons made their residence was erected by Ellis in 1704 and is still standing on the old farm. Harrison added many improvements to the estate and gave it the name of "Harriton." He began the culture of tobacco on a very large scale, having brought his slaves from Maryland to perform the labor.[5] Traditions say that the slaves soon became discontented and wanted to return to the South. They formed a scheme to poison the Harrison family and then make good their escape, but it seems that Providence interfered on behalf of the intended victims.

Richard Harrison was a man of intense religious zeal, and in 1730, he had erected on his plantation a small meeting house, which was used by the family and neighbors as a place of worship for many years. Nearby was the family cemetery, and Harrison made the following provision in his will for this, as well as the meeting house.

> And, whereas, I have erected a certain meeting-house or place of worship on part of my said tract of land In Merion township aforesaid; now, therefore, it is my will, and I do hereby declare that the said meeting-house, together with a square piece of ground containing, by estimation, two acres at least, adjoining to said house, where several of my children lie interred, shall not be sold by my said trustees, but that the same house and ground shall forever hereafter be exempted and reserved out of my said tract of land in Merion aforesaid, and shall remain and continue to be for use and service of a meeting-house and place of interment.

Hannah Harrison, who married Charles Thomson, was born at Harriton in 1728. After her father died in 1747, the family removed

---

5. This, in pre-Revolutionary days, was the residence of one Harrison, the proprietor of a slave plantation; for, little as we may care to acknowledge it, human slavery once existed in Pennsylvania, and in Lower Merion. Harrison's ambition was to hold a hundred slaves, but he was never permitted to realize this, as the hundredth always died, leaving him but ninety-nine. The souls of Harrison's slaves are said to haunt the whole Harriton domain."—"Something About Lower Merion," by Mrs. Margaret B. Harvey, in Collections of the Historical Society of Montgomery County, Pa., Vol. 1, p. 148.

to Somerville, near Philadelphia. During the Revolution, Thomson and his wife resided in his old home located at the corner of Spruce and Fourth Streets; but after resigning his position in Congress, he retired to Harriton, there to make an important contribution to literature. Like Jefferson, he was fond of agriculture, and, at the same time, he found the leisure to indulge his taste for reading. Timothy Pickering visited Thomson at Harriton, in December 1789, soon after his removal there, and he made the following observations:

> I had not been at Belmont for six weeks till last Sunday. I lodged there, and the next day, Mr. Peters and I went to see Charles Thomson, who lives six or seven miles above him. He was very glad to see us. We dined there. He has fitted up a small stone house very neatly and has a fine farm of six hundred acres, on which he intends to live the residue of his days. It is in bad order, owing to its having been many years in the hands of tenants. It will take him the rest of his life to bring it into complete order; but this, though attended with trouble, will be a constant source of pleasure; for nothing is so agreeable, nothing excites perpetual cheerfulness, like improvements growing up under our own care and management.[6]

---

6. The Life of Timothy Pickering, Vol. 2, p. 436.

chapter ten

Personal Character—Last Days at Harriton

lthough free from the cares of public life, Thomson continued to take an active interest in his country's welfare. His share in the struggle for Independence had been so great that he could not be indifferent to preserving the new Republic. He was conscious, too, of the many insidious and dangerous enemies that were menacing the liberties so dearly won; but he never despaired of the ultimate triumph of free institutions, and, in 1809, he wrote: "I hope the same kind of Providence which conducted us through the arduous struggle, will still continue to preserve."

He was opposed to the War of 1812, at the close of which, he remarked: "I read the newspapers for amusement and glance over the debates of the sages and am sorry to say I find more to disgust than to please."

Thomson was a man of cheerful temper, and his happiest hours were those spent in conversation with his friends. He was endowed with a large share of natural sagacity, which enabled him to understand men's motives and characters. He took a deep interest in the welfare of those just entering upon the duties of life. This is shown in a letter to Isaac Norris, a near relative of Mrs. Thomson, who went to France in 1784. Thomson's letter is filled with a true spirit of affection and reads as follows:

Philadelphia, June 19, 1784.

Dear Isaac,

I am pleased to hear of your safe arrival at Paris and hope the reception you met from our ministers was agreeable and satisfactory. I trust your good sense will dictate the obligations you are under to conduct yourself in such manner as to secure their favor and protection and do honor to my recommendation. You are now in the situation of Hercules, just stepping into life and left to yourself to follow unrestrained where passion leads, or prudence points the way. Before you, lie the rough ascent of virtue on the one hand, and the flowery path of pleasure on the other. I hope and trust you will with him make the glorious choice.

I have mentioned you in my letter to Mr. Jefferson, who, I expect will be arrived at Paris before this reaches you. You will wait upon him with my compliments. Cultivate his friendship, which you will find both useful and agreeable. I need not recommend to you a particular attention to all our ministers. I trust your conduct will merit their notice and convince them that you consider them as your patrons, which will be pleasing and honorable to you. Your mother, brother, and sister, and all friends are well. Mrs. T. joins in love to you. I am,

Dear Isaac,

Your affectionate,

Charles Thomson

At the same time, Thomson wrote a letter to John Jay and Jefferson, asking them to take young Norris under their protection. The letter to Mr. Jay is particularly interesting, as in it Thomson makes the following reference to his young friend:

He had the misfortune to lose his father and his uncle, who was his guardian, and who would have been a faithful guide to him, at an early age, and, therefore, has suffered in his education. I wished him to have spent a few years more in visiting his own country before he went abroad but found his inclination too strong to be resisted. I most heartily wish and fondly hope that by your advice he may be enabled to make the choice of Hercules. Should a contrary disposition unfortunately prevail, I wish you to use your influence to induce him to return home as soon as possible.

It appears that Jay and Jefferson both complied with Thomson's request and frequently gave advice to Mr. Norris, although they were thoroughly convinced that the influences of Paris were not the best for him. Jefferson expressed his views on the subject to Thomson as follows: "Indeed, from what I have seen here, I know not one good purpose on earth which can be effected by a young gentleman coming here. He may learn indeed to speak the language but put this in the scale amongst other things he will learn and evils he is sure to acquire, and it will be found too light. I have always disapproved of a European education for our youth from theory; I now do it from inspection."

It is scarcely necessary to make any further reference to Thomson's religious belief. He had accepted Christianity's truths in his early youth, and his whole life displayed a beautiful, upright character that was a constant inspiration to his friends. He not only became a Christian in the usual sense of the term, but he retired from public life, and for twenty-five years, was a solitary student of divine truth. Some have called him a Presbyterian; others insist that he inclined towards the Friends, while a few claim that he worshiped with the Baptists in later years. He declared while translating the Bible that "Attached to no system nor peculiar tenets of any sect or party, I have sought for truth with the utmost ingenuity."

He was a man of truth in all things, and his beautiful rendition of the thirteenth chapter of First Corinthians shows that he was a Christian who believed in the new commandment of Christ, "That ye love one another."

A traveler visiting Thomson at Harriton in 1822 found him engaged in reading aloud from *Young's Night Thoughts*. The visitor related that he was "Charmed at the distinct, audible, emphatic, appropriate and feeling manner with which the grand old man pronounced one of the finest passages in that admired author."

This same gentleman mentioned to Thomson the name of one of his Revolutionary associates, who had held a department under the order of the old Congress. Thomson recollected him very well and remarked: "Tell him I wish him prosperity and happiness, peace with God and peace with the world. Tell him to bear lightly on the world. Money, money, money is the god of the world."[7]

Thomson was a man of striking personal appearance, at least six feet tall, and he looked quite venerable, even before arriving at middle age. In 1781, Abbé Claude C. Robin, a chaplain in the Comte de Rochambeau's army, wrote of Thomson, as follows: "Among others Charles Thomson, Secretary of Congress, the soul of that political body, came also to receive and present his compliments. His meagre figure, furrowed countenance, and his hollow, sparkling eyes, his white straight hair, that did not hang quiet as low as his ears, fixed our thorough attention and filled us with surprise and admiration.[8]

In 1816, Thomson's health was considerably weakened by the infirmities of old age. Earlier in life, he had been brought to the gates of death several times by bilious complaints and fever, but in each case, he fully recovered his physical strength and the powers of his mind. In 1816, he wrote to Jefferson, describing his condition as follows:

> I find as I advance in life, that disorders of any kind make more
> lasting impressions. They chill the senses and stupefy the mind
> so as to render it incapable of exercising its powers. I have parted
> with most of my teeth, and the few stumps that remain are unfit
> for mastication. My eyes indeed (though in 1778 I almost lost

---

7. Berks and Schuylkill Journal, August 24, 1822.
8. Life and Correspondence of Joseph Reed, Vol. 2, p. 307.

the use of them by what the French call a *coup de soleil)* have been so far restored that I write and read without spectacles, and use them only occasionally to ease the eyes when tired or when the print is too small. My hearing is so dull that I can take no share in common conversation, so that when my friends visit me and wish to communicate anything or ask me a question, they must sit near me and bawl. My memory is like a riddle. But why should I proceed with this detail of weaknesses? How few at my age enjoy greater comforts! I am free from gout or stone or any acute disorder. My sleep is sweet, and when tired by day or night I can by laying my head on a pillow, enjoy that comfort.

Sometime during the year 1816, Thomson had a paralytic stroke, which seriously affected the powers of his mind. This was soon followed by a second attack, leaving him physically helpless. He remained in this condition until November 1816, when his recovery came on as suddenly as the attacks he had received. His wife died on September 6, 1807, and in his declining years, he was cared for by his nephew, John Thomson, and his maiden sister, Mary, who made her home with him. John F. Watson visited Thomson in April 1824 and made the following observations: "I found him still the erect, tall man he had ever been; his countenance very little changed, but his mental faculties in ruins. He could not remember me, although formerly an occasional visitor. He appeared cheerful, and with many smiles, expressed thankfulness for the usual expressions of kindness extended to him. Charles Thomson passed most of his time reposing and slumbering on a settee in the common parlor. A circumstance occurred at the dinner table, at the head of which he was usually placed, which sufficiently marked the aberration of his mind, even while it showed that 'his very failings leaned to virtue's side.' While the grace was saying by a clergyman present, he began in an elevated and audible voice to say the Lord's prayer, and he did not desist, nor regard the other, although his grace was also saying at the same time. It was remarkable that his prayer was all said in the words of his own translation and with entire correctness. He made no remarks at the table and ate without discrimination whatever was set before him."[9]

Thomson had frequently expressed the belief that he would live to the age of one hundred years. His life was prolonged to almost a century, for he died on August 16, 1824, at ninety-five years. His remains were deposited in the family cemetery, about a quarter of a mile southeast of the mansion. On the wall may be found the following inscription:

Harriton Family Cemetery, Anno 1719. This stone is opposite the division between two rows of family graves, wherein were interred

RICHARD HARRISON
(Died March 2, 1747)
And a number of his descendants,
Also
CHARLES THOMSON,
Secretary of the Continental Congress,
Died August 16, 1824,
And
HANNAH THOMSON,
Wife of Charles Thomson, daughter of Richard Harrison, grand-daughter of Isaac Norris and great-granddaughter of Governor Thomas Lloyd,
Died Sept. 6, 1807.

Providence favored all of Thomson's immediate relatives with a great length of years. On the flyleaf of a copy of the *Synopsis of the Four Evangelists* in Allegheny College Library is the following record:

1. John Thomson, the Father.
2. William died at the age of 93.
3. Alexander died at the age of 80.

---

9. Watson's Annals of Philadelphia and Pennsylvania, Vol. 2, p. 570

4. Charles died at the age of 95—by three months.

5. Matthew died at the age of 91.

6. John died at the age of 79.

7. Mary in her 84th year.

The above, children of John Thomson first named, who died within the capes of the Delaware. Information from Mr. John Thomson, son of Alexander, as obtained by Timothy Alden, First President of Allegheny College.

By the terms of Charles Thomson's will, he bequeathed his estate to his nephew, John Thomson, subject to the maintenance of his aged sister, Mary, during her natural life. John Thomson thus acquired possession of all his uncle's valuable papers, as well as the silver urn presented to him by Congress. The further disposal of these papers has been referred to in another part of this volume, while the silver urn passed into the hands of Charles T. Chamberlain, who married one of John Thomson's daughters. The estate at Harriton was disposed of in 1798, before the death of Charles Thomson's wife. In that year, she executed with her husband a deed by which, after reserving a life estate for themselves, Harriton was settled upon Charles McClenachan, a grandson of Mrs. Thomson's brother, Thomas Harrison. Young McClenachan was a great favorite in the Thomson family and was brought up and educated at Harriton. The deeds were loosely drawn, and on McClenachan's death in 1811, the question of title was disputed among his heirs; but the property was finally settled upon his daughter, Naomi. She afterward married Levi Morris, and their descendants own the estate to this day.

In 1838, the remains of Charles Thomson were disturbed from their repose in the tomb of Harriton. Early in this century, trouble arose because certain citizens of Lower Merion desired to get possession of the cemetery for public use.[10] They even went so far as to petition the Legislature but in vain. After a series of annoyances, the owners remained

10. Pennsylvania Magazine of History and Biography, Vol. 15, p. 212; also, Collections of the Historical Society of Montgomery County, Pa., Vol. I, p. 394.

in undisputed possession, until 1838, when the promoters of Laurel Hill Cemetery, Philadelphia, made proposals to the Harriton heirs to remove the bodies of Charles Thomson and wife to Laurel Hill. John Thomson claimed the authority to remove his uncle's remains, but as the Harriton heirs refused to grant permission, the matter was dropped for a time. One night, however, in the latter part of the year 1838, the remains were dug up, hurriedly thrust into a wagon, and driven off to Laurel Hill. A tomb was provided in one of the cemetery's fairest spots, overlooking the Schuylkill, and a plain monument sixteen feet high marks the place. At the foot of the monument are two marble slabs, one of them containing the following inscription:

Erected by John Thomson, of Delaware, to the memory of an
Honored uncle and benefactor,
Also
In Memory of
HANNAH,
Wife of Charles Thomson,
Born December 1, 1731,
Died September 6, 1807.
CHARLES
Son of John Thomson,
Born January 17, 1795,
Died March 26, 1820.
Removed from Lower Merion, Pennsylvania, 1838.

The other slab contains the following inscription, composed by John F. Watson:

This monument
Covers the remains of the
HONOURABLE
CHARLES THOMSON,
The first, and long

The Confidential Secretary of the
Continental Congress,
And the
Enlightened benefactor of his country
In its day of period and need.
Born November 29, 1729,
Died August 16, 1824.
Full of honours and of years.

As a Patriot
His memorial and just honours
Are inscribed on the pages
Of his country's history

————

As a Christian,
His piety was sincere and enduring,
His Biblical learning was profound,
As is shown by his translation of the Septuagint.
As a Man,
He was honored, loved and wept.

————

Erected
To the memory of an honoured
Uncle and Benefactor,
By his Nephew,
John Thomson, of Delaware.

————

Hic Jacet
Homo veritatis et gratiæ

Charles Thomson

Charles Thomson Memorial in Laurel Hill Cemetery
The plaque reads: Charles Thomson (1729 – 1824) First and only secretary to the
Continental and Confederation Congresses (1774 – 1789) A farmer and biblical
scholar in retirement at his estate called Harriton in Bryn Mawr.

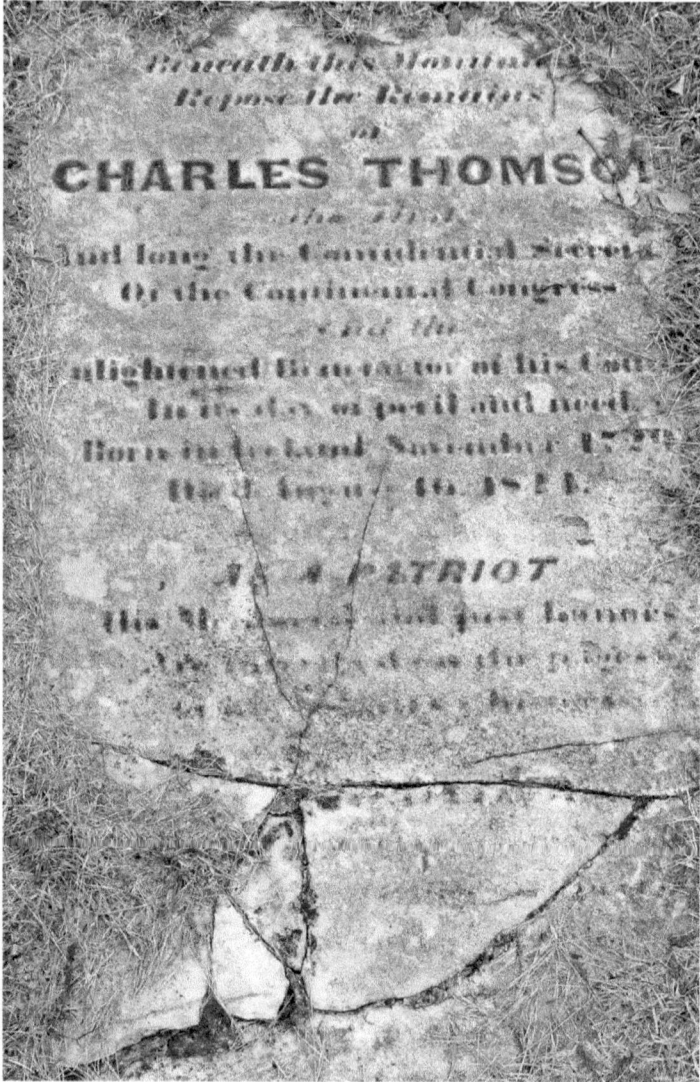

One of the stone slabs at the foot of the Charles Thomson Memorial

Bibliography

The following are the most important papers and writings left by Charles Thomson:

- The earliest of the Thomson papers in 1765. He had begun his observations on passing events at the time of the Stamp Act Congress and wrote a record of its doings, which William B. Reed, in a discourse, before the New York Historical Society, December 19, 1839, said was in his possession. It is printed in the New York Historical Society publications for 1878. The papers of the Continental Congress passed from Thomson's hands into those of Roger Alden for safekeeping, by order of Washington, July 24, 1789. Theodore F. Dwight describes them in his paper on "The Authentication of the Declaration of Independence," Cambridge, 1885. The "Rough Journals," September 5, 1774-March 2, 1789, are the original minutes, contained in thirty-nine foolscap volumes. Of this, for the interval September 5, 1775-January 20, 1779, there is a fair copy in ten volumes, and the published journals were printed from this copy. A third journal is the "Secret Domestic Journal," May 10, 1775-October 26, 1787. A fourth is a "Secret Journal Foreign and Domestic," October 18, 1780-March 29, 1786. A fifth is "Secret Journal of Foreign Affairs," November 29, 1775-September 16, 1788, in three volumes. A sixth is an "Imperfect Secret Journal," September 17, 1776-September 16, 1788. A seventh is the "More Secret Journal," in which there are few entries. An eighth is a "Secret Journal A," 1776-1783, being minutes afterward entered in the public journals. —*Windsor's Narrative and Critical History, Vol. 8.*

- Six pages in the handwriting and with the autograph of Charles Thomson appended to extracts of Congress relative to Prizes and Privateers. —In the Library of the Historical Society of Pennsylvania.

- Manuscript translation of the Septuagint. —In the Library of Allegheny College, Meadville, Pa.

- Manuscript translation of the New Testament. —In the Library of the Historical Society of Pennsylvania.

- Manuscript notebook used in translating the New Testament. —In the Library of the Historical Society of Pennsylvania.

- Manuscript account book, 1815-1816. —In the Library of the Historical Society of Pennsylvania.

- Manuscript letter book. —In the Library of the Historical Society of Pennsylvania.

- Minute book of the American Philosophical Society for the years 1769 and 1770. —In the Library of the Society, Philadelphia.

- *The Holy Bible, Containing the Old and New Covenant, Commonly Called the Old and New Testament* translated from Greek, by Charles Thomson. —Printed by Jane Aitkens, No. 71 North Third Street, Philadelphia, 1808.

- *A Synopsis of the Four Evangelists*, by Charles Thomson, Philadelphia: Published for the Author. William McCulloch, Printer, 1815.

- *An Enquiry into the Causes of the Alienation of the Delaware and Shawenese Indians from the British Interest*, by Charles Thomson. London, 1759.

- "An Essay Upon Indian Affairs."—*Memoirs of the Historical Society of Pennsylvania*. Vol. I, p. 80, Philadelphia, 1853.

The following works were consulted in the preparation of this volume:

Adams: *The works of John Adams, Second President of the United States, with a Life of the Author* by His Grandson, Charles Francis Adams. 10 vols. Boston: Little, Brown and Company, 1852.

Adolphus: *The History of England from the Accession of King George the Third to the Conclusion of Peace in 1783* by John Adolphus. London: T. Cadell and W. Davies, 1810.

Alexander: *Biographical Sketches of the Founder and Principal Alumni of the Log College* by A. Alexander, D. D. Princeton: Printed by J. T. Robinson, 1845.

American historical association: "Annual Report for the year 1892." Washington: Government Printing Office, 1893.

——— "Annual Report for the year 1894." Washington: Government Printing Office, 1895.

——— "Annual Report for the year 1896." Washington: Government Printing Office, 1897.

American Quarterly Review: Volume I. Philadelphia: Carey, Lea and Carey, 1827.

Armor: *Lives of the Governors of Pennsylvania* by William C. Armor. Philadelphia: James K. Simon, 1872.

Auge: *Lives of the Eminent Dead and Biographical Notices of Prominent Living Citizens of Montgomery Co., Pa.* by M. Auge. Published by the Author. Norristown, Pa., 1879.

Baker: *Washington After the Revolution, 1784-1799* by William Spohn Baker. J. B. Lippincott Company, Philadelphia, 1898.

Bancroft: *History of the United States of America, From the Discovery of the Continent* by George Bancroft. 6 vols. New York: D. Appleton and Company, 1889.

Bean: *History of Montgomery County, Pennsylvania* edited by Theodore W. Bean. Philadelphia: Everts and Peck, 1884.

Berks and Schuylkill Journal: August 24, 1822. Reading, Pa.

Bigelow: *The Life of Benjamin Franklin, Written by Himself, Now First Edited from Original Sources and from His Printed Correspondence and Other Writings* by John Bigelow. 3 vols. Philadelphia: J. B. Lippincott and Co., 1874.

Bishop: *A History of American Manufactures* by J. Leander Bishop, M.D. 3 vols. Philadelphia: Edward Young and Company, 1861.

Brotherhead: *The Book of the Signers, Containing Fac Simile Letters of the Signers of the Declaration of Independence* edited by William Brotherhead. Philadelphia: William Brotherhead, 1861.

Buchanan: *Life of Hon. Thomas McKean, Compiled for the Genealogy of the McKean Family* by Roberdeau Buchanan. Lancaster, Pa: Inquirer Printing Co., 1890.

Buck: *History of the Indian Walk Performed for the Proprietaries of Pennsylvania in 1737* by William J. Buck, Philadelphia: Edwin S. Stuart, 1886.

Carson: *History of the Celebration of the One Hundredth Anniversary of the Promulgation of the Constitution of the United States* by Hampton L. Carson. 2 vols. Philadelphia: J. B. Lippincott Company, 1889.

Cathcart: *The Baptist Encyclopedia* by William Cathcart, D.D. Philadelphia: Louis H. Everts, 1881.

Chamberlain: *John Adams, the Statesman of the American Revolution, with Other Essays and Addresses Historical and Literacy* by Mellen Chamberlain, LL.D. Boston and New York: Houghton, Mifflin & Co., 1898.

Chambers: *A Tribute to the Principles, Virtues, Habits, and Public Usefulness of the Irish and Scotch Early Settlers in Pennsylvania* by George Chambers. Chambersburg, Pa.: Printed by M. Kieffer & Co., 1856.

Collections of the Massachusetts Historical Society: For the Year 1795. Boston: Printed by Samuel Hall, 1795. Reprinted by John H. Eastburn, 1835.

Custis: *Recollections and Private Memoirs of Washington* by His Adopted Son, George Washington Parke Custis. New York: Published by Derby & Jackson, 1860.

Day: *Historical Collections of the State of Pennsylvania* by Sherman Day. Philadelphia: George W. Gorton, 1843.

Debates and Proceedings in the Congress of the United States: Vol. I. Compiled by Joseph Gales, Sr. Washington: Printed and published by Gales & Seaton, 1834.

Dubois: *A Discourse on the Origin and History of the Presbyterian Church Congregation of New London, in Chester County, Pennsylvania* by the Pastor Robert P. Du Bois. Philadelphia: King & Baird Printers, 9 George street, 1845.

———— *Historical Discourse Delivered on the Occasion of the One Hundred and Fiftieth Anniversary of the New London Presbyterian Church, Chester, Co., Pa., June 22, 1876* by the Pastor, Rev. Robert P. Du Bois, Oxford, PA: The Press Job Printing Office, 1876.

Egle: *An Illustrated History of the Commonwealth of Pennsylvania* by William H. Egle, M.D. Harrisburg: De Witt C. Goodrich, 1877.

Fisher: *Pennsylvania, Colony and Commonwealth* by Sydney George Fisher. Philadelphia: Henry T. Coates and Company, 1897.

———— *The Making of Pennsylvania* by Sydney George Fisher. Philadelphia: J. B. Lippincott Company, 1898.

Fiske: *The American Revolution* by John Fiske. 2 vols. Boston and New York: Houghton, Mifflin, and Co., 1891.

Friedenwald: *The Continental Congress, in the Annual Report of the American Historical Association for the Year 1894.* Washington: Government Printing Office, 1895.

———— *The Journals and Papers of the Continental Congress, in the Annual Report of the American Historical Association for the Year 1896.* Washington: Government Printing Office, 1897.

Frothingham: *The Rise of the Republic of the United States* by Richard Frothingham. Fifth Edition. Boston: Little, Brown and Company, 1890.

Froude: *The English in Ireland in the Eighteenth Century* by James Anthony Froude, M.A. 2 vols. New York: Scribner, Armstrong, and Co., 1873.

Futhey: *History of Chester County, Pennsylvania, With Genealogical and Biographical Sketches* by J. S. Futhey and Gilbert Cope. Philadelphia: Louis H. Everts, 1881.

———— *Discourse Delivered on the Occasion of the One Hundred and Fiftieth Anniversary of the Upper Octoraro Presbyterian Church, Chester County, Pennsylvania, Sept. 14, 1870* by J. Smith Futhey, Esq. Philadelphia: Henry B. Ashmead, 1870.

Galloway: *Historical and Political Reflections on the Rise and Progress of the American Revolution* by Joseph Galloway. London: Printed for G. Wilkie, 1780.

Gazette of the United States: July 25, 1789.

Goodloe: *The Birth of the Republic*; by Daniel R. Goodloe. Chicago, New York and San Francisco: Belford, Clarke, and Co.

Gordon: *The History of Pennsylvania, From Its Discovery by Europeans to the Declaration of Independence in 1776* by Thomas F. Gordon. Philadelphia: Carey, Lea, and Carey, 1829.

Gough: *A History of the People Called Quakers, From Their First Rise to the Present Time* by John Gough. 3 vols. Dublin: Printed for Robert Jackson, 1789.

Graydon: *Memoirs of a Life Passed in Pennsylvania Within the Last Sixty Years* by Alexander Graydon. Harrisburg: Printed by John Wyeth, 1811. A fine edition of this book was published in Edinburgh, 1822, by William Blackwood.

Greene: *Historical View of the American Revolution* by George Washington Greene. Boston: Ticknor and Fields, 1865.

Grimshaw: *History of the United States from Their First Settlement as Colonies to the Period of the Fifth Census in 1830* by William Grimshaw. Philadelphia: Grigg and Elliott, 1842.

Hale: *History of the United States from Their First Settlement as Colonies to the Close of the War with Great Britain in 1815* by Hon. Salma Hale. London: John Miller, 50 Pall Mall, 1827.

Handy: *Newark, Delaware: Past and Present* by Egbert G. Handy and James L. Vallandigham, Jr.

Harding: "Party Struggles Over the First Pennsylvania Constitution," in the *Annual Report of the American Historical Association for the Year 1894*. Washington: Government Printing Office, 1895.

Harley: *Charles Thomson, Patriot and Scholar* by Lewis R. Harley, Ph.D., Norristown, Pa. The Historical Society of Montgomery Co., 1897.

Hart: *American History Told by Contemporaries* by Albert Bushnell Hart. Vol. II. New York: The Macmillan Company, 1898.

Haverford College: *A History of Haverford College for the First Sixty Years of its Existence* prepared by a Committee of the Alumni Association. Philadelphia: Porter and Coates, 1892.

Henry: *Patrick Henry, Life, Correspondence and Speeches* by William Wirt Henry. 3 vols. New York: Charles Scribner's Sons, 1891.

Hildreth: *The History of the United States* by Richard Hildreth. 6 vols. New York: Harper and Brothers, 1880.

Historical Sketches: *A Collection of Papers Prepared for the Historical Society of Montgomery County, Pennsylvania* Vol. I. Published by the Society. Norristown, Pa., 1895.

Holmes: *American Annals or a Chronological History of America, from its Discovery in 1492 to 1806* by Abiel Holmes, D.D. 2 vols. Cambridge: Printed and Sold by W. Hilliard, 1805.

———— *The Life of Ezra Stiles, D.D., LL.D.* by Abiel Holmes, A.M. Boston: Thomas and Andrews, 1798.

Horne: *A Manual of Biblical Bibliography, Comprising a Catalogue Methodically Arranged of the Principal Editions and Versions of the Holy Scriptures* by Thomas Hartwell Horne, B.D., of St. John's College, Cambridge, London: T. Cadell, Strand, 1839.

Hosack: *A Biographical Memoir of Hugh Williamson, M.D., LL.D., Delivered November 1, 1819, at the Request of the New York Historical Society* by David Hosack published in the Collections of the New York Historical Society, 1821.

Howison: *A History of the United States of America* by Robert Reid Howison. Richmond, Virginia: Everett Waddey Company, 1892.

Hudson: *Journalism in the United States, from 1690 to 1872* by Frederic Hudson. New York: Harper and Brothers, 1873.

Huffington: *The Delaware Register and Farmers' Magazine, from February to July 1838* edited by William Huffington, Dover, Delaware: S. Kimmey, Printer, 1838.

Jay: *The Life of John Jay, with Selections from His Correspondence* by His Son, William Jay. 2 vols. New York: Printed and Published by J. and J. Harper, 1833.

Jefferson: *Notes on the State of Virginia* written by Thomas Jefferson; London: Printed for John Stockdale, 1787.

Jones: *The Life of Ashbel Green* by Joseph H. Jones. New York: Robert Carter and Brothers, 1849.

Lewis: *A History of the Bank of North America* by Lawrence Lewis, Jr. Philadelphia: J. B. Lippincott Company, 1882.

Lossing: *Pictorial Field Book of the Revolution* by Benson J. Lossing. 2 vols. New York: Harper and Brothers, Franklin Square.

——— *Seventeen Hundred and Seventy-Six, or the War of Independence* by Benson J. Lossing. New York: Edward Walker, 1847.

——— *The Home of Washington, or Mt. Vernon and its Associations* by Benson J. Lossing, Hartford, Connecticut: A. S. Hale & Co., 1870.

Maclay: *Journal of William Maclay, United States Senator from Pennsylvania, 1789-1791* edited by Edgar S. Maclay, A.M. New York: D. Appleton & Company, 1890.

——— *Sketches of Debate in the First Senate of the United States, 1789-90-91* by William Maclay. Edited by Geo. W. Harris, Harrisburg: Lane S. Hart, Printer and Binder.

Madison: *Letters and Other Writings of James Madison* published by order of Congress. 4 vols. Philadelphia: J. B. Lippincott Company, 1865.

Marshall: *Passages from the Diary of Christopher Marshall, Kept in Philadelphia During the American Revolution* edited by William Duane. Philadelphia: Hazard and Mitchell, No. 178 Chestnut Street, 1838.

Marshall: *The Life of Washington* by John Marshall. Second Edition. Philadelphia: James Crissy, 1838.

Martin: *Chester and its Vicinity, Delaware County, in Pennsylvania* by John Hill Martin, Esq. Philadelphia, 1887.

——— *Historical Sketch of Bethlehem, with Some Account of the Moravian Church* by John Hill Martin. Philadelphia: John L. Pile, No. 422 Walnut Street, 1873.

Miller: *A Brief Retrospect of the Eighteenth Century* by Samuel Miller, A.M. New York: Printed by T. and J. Swords, 1803.

Minutes of the Provincial Congress and the Council of Safety of the State of New Jersey. Trenton: Printed by Naar, Day, and Naar, 1879.

Mittelberger: *Journey to Pennsylvania in the year 1750 and Return to Germany in the year 1754* by Gottlieb Mittelberger. Translated from the German by Carl Theo. Eben. Philadelphia: John Jos. McVey, 1898.

Moon: *The Morris Family of Philadelphia, Descendants of Anthony Morris 1654-1721* by Robert C. Moon, M.D. 3 vols. Philadelphia: Robert C. Moon, 1319 Walnut St., 1898.

Moore: *Diary of the American Revolution, from Newspapers and Original Documents* by Frank Moore, 2 vols. New York: Charles Scribner, 1859.

———— *Materials for History Printed from Original Manuscripts with Notes and Illustrations* by Frank Moore. New York: Printed for the Zenger Club, 1861.

Moore: *The American Congress, a History of National Legislation and Political Events, 1774-1895* by Joseph West Moore. New York: Harper and Brothers, 1895.

Morse: *Benjamin Franklin in American Statemen Series* by John T. Morse, Jr. Boston and New York: Houghton, Mifflin, and Company, 1889.

New Jersey Archives: First Series, Vols. 10, 11, 12 and 19 edited by Frederick W. Record and William Nelson. Newark, N.J., 1886.

New York Historical Society Collections Vol. III. New York: Published by E. Bliss and E. White, 128 Broadway, 1821.

———— *For the year 1878*, containing the Thomson Papers. New York: Printed for the Society, 1879.

Niles: *Weekly Register, Containing Political, Historical, Geographical, Scientific, Statistical, Economical and Biographical documents, Essays and Facts* by H. Niles, Editor. Vol. 25. Baltimore: Printed by William Ogden Niles.

———— *Principles and Acts of the Revolution in America* New Edition: A. S. Barnes and Co., New York, 1876.

Odell: See Joseph Stansbury.

Patton: *A Concise History of the American People* by Jacob Harris Patton, A.M. New York: Fords, Howard, and Hulbert, 1882.

Pearse: *A Concise History of the Iron Manufacture of the American Colonies up to the Revolution* by John B. Pearse, A.M. Philadelphia: Allen, Lane, and Scott, 1876.

Pennsylvania Archives: Second Series Vol 3; edited by John B. Linn and Wm. H. Egle, M.D. Harrisburg: E. K. Meyers, State Printer, 1890.

Pennsylvania Magazine of History and Biography Vol. 15. Philadelphia: The Historical Society of Pennsylvania, 1891.

Pennsylvania Packet and Daily Advertiser, April 28, 30, and May 5, 1789.

Pitkin: *A Political and Civil History of the United States of America* by Timothy Pitkin. 2 vols. New Haven: Published by Hezekiah Howe and Durrie and Peck, 1828.

Powell: *The History of Education in Delaware* by Lyman P. Powell, A.B. Washington: Government Printing Office, 1893.

Proceedings of the Massachusetts Historical Society, 1860-1862. Boston: Printed for the Society, 1862.

Ramsay: *History of the United States from their First Settlement as English Colonies in 1607, to the year 1808* by David Ramsay, M.D. Continued to the Treaty of Ghent, by S. S. Smith, D.D., and other literary gentlemen. 3 vols. Philadelphia: Published by M. Carey, 1816.

Randall: *The Life of Thomas Jefferson* by Henry S. Randall, LL.D. 3 vols. New York: Derby and Jackson, 1858.

Randolph: *Memoir, Correspondence, and Miscellanies, from the Papers of Thomas Jefferson* by Thomas Jefferson Randolph. 2 vols. Charlottesville: F. Carr and Co., 1829.

Rayner: *Life of Thomas Jefferson, with Selections from the Most Valuable Portions of his Voluminous and Unrivalled Correspondence* by B. L. Raynor. Boston: Lilly, Wait, Colman and Holden, 1834.

Reed: *Life and Correspondence of Joseph Reed* by his Grandson, William B. Reed. 2 vols. Philadelphia: Lindsay and Blakiston, 1847.

Reichel: *Memorials of the Moravian Church* edited by William E. Reichel. Vol. I. Philadelphia: J. B. Lippincott & Co., 1870.

Richardson: *A Compilation of the Messages and Papers of the Presidents, 1789-1897* published by Authority of Congress. Edited by James D. Richardson. 10 vols. Washington: Government Printing Office, 1896-1900.

Robins: *Benjamin Franklin, in American Men of Energy Series* by Edward Robins. New York and London: G. P. Putnam's Sons, 1898.

Rupp: *History of Northampton, Lehigh, Monroe, Carbon and Schuylkill Counties* by I. Daniel Rupp. Harrisburg: Hickock and Cantine, Printers, 1845.

Sabine: *Biographical Sketches of Loyalists of the American Revolution, with an Historical Essay* by Lorenzo Sabine. 2 vols. Boston: Little, Brown and Company, 1864.

Sargent: *The History of an Expedition Against Fort Du Quesne in 1755* by Winthrop Sargent. Philadelphia: J. B. Lippincott & Co., 1856.

Scharf: *History of Delaware from 1609-1888* by J. Thomas Scharf, A.M., LL.D. 2 vols. Philadelphia: L. J. Richards and Co., 1888.

——— *The Chronicles of Baltimore* by J. Thomas Scharf. Baltimore: Turnbull Bros., 1874.

——— *History of Maryland from the Earliest Period to the Present Day* by J. Thomas Scharf. 3 vols. Baltimore: Published by John B. Piet, 1879.

——— *History of Philadelphia, 1608-1884* by J. Thomas Scharf and Thompson Westcott. 3 vols. Philadelphia: L. H. Everts and Co., 1884.

Sharpless: *A Quaker Experiment in Government* by Isaac Sharpless. Philadelphia: Alfred J. Ferris, 1898.

Simpson: *The Lives of Eminent Philadelphians Now Deceased. Collected from Original and Authentic Sources* by Henry Simpson. Philadelphia: William Brotherhead, 1859.

Smith: *The Friend: A Religious and Literary Journal* by Robert Smith. Vol. I. Philadelphia: John Richardson, 1829.

Smyth: *The Philadelphia Magazines and their Contributors, 1741-1850* by Albert H. Smyth. Philadelphia: Robert M. Lindsay, 1892.

Sparks: *The Life and Writings of Benjamin Franklin* by Jared Sparks. 10 vols. Philadelphia: Childs and Peterson, 1840.

——— *The Life of George Washington* by Jared Sparks. Boston: Little, Brown and Co., 1857.

——— *The Writings of George Washington, with a Life of the Author* by Jared Sparks. 12 vols. Boston: Russell, Shattuck and Williams, 1836.

Sprague: *Annals of the American Pulpit, or Commemorative Notices of Distinguished American Clergymen of Various Denominations* by William B. Sprague, D.D. Vol. III. New York: Robert Carter and Brothers, 1858.

Stanbury: *The Loyal Verses of Joseph Stansbury and Jonathan Odell* edited by Winthrop Sargent. Albany: J. Munsell, 78 State Street, 1860.

Sumner: *Alexander Hamilton, in Makers of America Series* by William G. Sumner, LL.D. New York: Dodd, Mead and Company, 1890.

————— *The Financier, and the Finances of the American Revolution* by William G. Sumner, LL.D. 2 vols. New York: Dodd, Mead and Company, 1891.

Thomas: *A History of the United States* by Allen C. Thomas. Boston: D. C. Heath and Co., 1897.

Thomas: *Travels Through the Western Country* by David Thomas. Auburn, N. Y.: Printed by David Rumsey, 1819.

Thomas: *The History of Printing in America* by Isaiah Thomas, LL.D. 2 vols. Albany N.Y.: Joel Munsell, 1874.

Thomson: *Chester County and its People* edited by W. W. Thomson. Chicago and New York: The Union History Company, 1898.

Tyler: *Patrick Henry, in American Statesmen Series* by Moses Coit Tyler. Boston and New York: Houghton, Mifflin and Company, 1889.

Upham: *The Life of Timothy Pickering* by Charles W. Upham. 4 vols. Boston: Little, Brown and Company, 1873.

Vallandigham: *History of the Presbytery of New Castle from its Organization, March 13, 1717 to 1888* by Rev. J. L. Vallandigham, D.D., L.L.D., and Rev. Samuel A. Gayley, D.D. Philadelphia: Presbyterian Publishing Co.

Watson: *Annals of Philadelphia and Pennsylvania* by John F. Watson. 2 vols. Philadelphia: Published by Elijah Thomas, 1857.

Wells: *The Life and Public Services of Samuel Adams* by William V. Wells. 3 vols. Boston: Little, Brown and Co., 1888.

Wharton: *The Revolutionary Diplomatic Correspondence of the United States* by Francis Wharton. 6 vols. Washington: Government Printing Office, 1889.

Wickerman: *A History of Education in Pennsylvania* by James Pyle Wickerman, LL.D. Lancaster, Pa.: Inquirer Publishing Company, 1886.

Wiley: *Biographical and Portrait Cyclopedia of Montgomery County, Pennsylvania* edited by Samuel T. Wiley. Philadelphia: Biographical Publishing Company, 1895.

Winsor: *Narrative and Critical History of America* by Justin Winsor. 8 vols. Boston and New York: Houghton, Mifflin and Co., 1889.

————— *The Westward Movement; The Colonies and the Republic West of the Alleghenies, 1763-1898* by Justin Winsor. Boston and New York: Houghton, Mifflin and Co., 1897.

Wister: *Worthy Women of Our First Century* edited by Mrs. O. J. Wister and Miss Agnes Irwin. Philadelphia: J. B. Lippincott and Co., 1877.

Wood: *Early History of the University of Pennsylvania* by George B. Wood, M.D. Third Edition, with Supplementary Chapters by Frederick D. Stone. Litt. D. Philadelphia: J. B. Lippincott Co., 1896.

Wright: *Early Bibles of America* by Rev. John Wright, D.D. Third Edition. New York: Thomas Whittaker, 1894.

Index

About the Author

Lewis Reifsnyder Harley, Ph.D., (1866–1923), was born at North Coventry, Chester County, Pennsylvania, on August 16, 1866. His parents were Harrison and Sue Yarnell Harley. He began his training at the West Chester Normal School and studied at the Hill School in Pottstown, Pennsylvania. Granted a state certificate to teach by the Lock Haven Normal School in 1891, he taught in the country schools of Illinois and at the same time studied at Illinois Wesleyan University, where he received a Bachelor of Philosophy degree. The following year, he entered the University of Pennsylvania's graduate department and was awarded a Ph.D. in 1895.

Harley was principal at the North Wales High School for six years, and in 1896, entered the Central High School as a professor of history. He became head of that department in 1917 and served in that capacity until he was called to the Girls High School in 1921.

Harley held an honorary degree of Master of Arts from Dickinson College and Master of Philosophy from the University of Pittsburgh. He was a member of the American Historical Association, the Historical Society of Pennsylvania, and a vice president of the Classical Club of Philadelphia. Throughout his lifetime, he contributed to many journals.

.